**Stripe
Press**

Ideas for progress
San Francisco, California
press.stripe.com

Stubborn Attachments

A vision for a society of free, prosperous, and responsible individuals

Growth is good. Through history, economic growth in particular has alleviated human misery, improved human happiness and opportunity, and lengthened human lives. Wealthier societies are more stable, offer better living standards, produce better medicines, and ensure greater autonomy, greater fulfillment, and more sources of fun. If we want to sustain our trends of growth, and the overwhelmingly positive outcomes for societies that come with it, every individual must become more concerned with the welfare of those around us.

So, how do we proceed? Tyler Cowen, in a culmination of twenty years of thinking and research, provides a roadmap for moving forward. In this new book, *Stubborn Attachments: A Vision for a Society of Free, Prosperous, and Responsible Individuals*, Cowen argues that our reason and common sense can help free us of the faulty ideas that hold us back as people and as a society. *Stubborn Attachments*, at its heart, makes the contemporary moral case for economic growth, and in doing so delivers a great dose of inspiration and optimism about our future possibilities.

The author wishes to thank Agnes Callard, Bryan Caplan, Patrick Collison, David Gordon, Robin Hanson, Daniel Jacobson, Kevin McCabe, Sarah Oh, Meg Patrick, Derek Parfit, Hollis Robbins, Tom Round, Amni Rusli, David Schmidtz, Alex Tabarrok, Larry Temkin, University of Pennsylvania seminar participants, Kevin Vallier, and numerous commentators on earlier papers related to this work for useful comments and discussions. The Mercatus Center supplied useful research assistance. Special thanks go to my agent, Teresa Hartnett, to Brianna Wolfson for her work on the publishing side, to Tyler Thompson and Kevin Wong for the design of the book, to Rebecca Hiscott for editing, and to Patrick Collison for his interest in publishing this book with Stripe.

Tyler Cowen is a Holbert L. Harris Professor at George Mason University and Director of the Mercatus Center. He received his PhD in economics from Harvard University in 1987. His book *The Great Stagnation: How America Ate the Low-Hanging Fruit of Modern History, Got Sick, and Will (Eventually) Feel Better* was a *New York Times* best seller. He was recently named in an *Economist* poll as one of the most influential economists of the last decade, and several years ago *Bloomberg Businessweek* dubbed him "America's Hottest Economist." *Foreign Policy* magazine named him as one of its "Top 100 Global Thinkers" of 2011. He also cowrites a blog at marginalrevolution.com, runs a podcast series called "Conversations with Tyler," and has cofounded an online economics education project, mruniversity.com. His most recently published book was *The Complacent Class: The Self-Defeating Quest for the American Dream.*

Published in the United States of America
by Stripe Press / Stripe Matter Inc.

Stripe Press
Ideas for progress
San Francisco, California
press.stripe.com

Printed by Hemlock in Canada
ISBN: 978-1-7322651-3-4

First Edition

Table of contents

Tyler Cowen

Stubborn
Attachments

A vision for a society of free, prosperous,
and responsible individuals

When it comes to the future of our world, we have lost our way in a fundamental manner, and not just on a few details. We must return to principles, but we do not always have good principles to guide us. We have strayed from the ideals of a society based on prosperity and the rights and liberties of the individual, and we do not know how to return to those ideals.

It sounds so simple: prosperity and individual liberty. Who could be opposed to that? In the abstract, few people would speak out against those values. But in practice, we turn away from them all the time. We pursue many other ends, ones we should instead ignore or reject. We need to develop a tougher, more dedicated, and indeed a more stubborn attachment to prosperity and freedom. When you see what this means in practice, you may wince at some of the implications, and you may be put off by the moral absolutism it will require. Yet these goals—strictly rather than loosely pursued—are of historic importance for our civilization, and if we adhere to them, they will bring an enormous amount of good into our world.

But how do we know which goods we should be pursuing, and how do we weigh one value against another? How should we make decisions when moral values clash? These rather corny questions—the stuff of freshman bull sessions, presented and chewed over around the dorm—remain of vital import.

Before considering how to make such trade-offs, here is some background on my underlying philosophical stance and what I intend to bring to the table.

I treat questions of right and wrong as having correct answers, at least in principle. We should admit the existence of significant moral grey areas, but right and wrong are a kind of "natural fact," as many philosophers would say. To put it bluntly: there exists an objective right and an objective wrong. Relativism is a nonstarter, and most people are not sincere in their relativist pronouncements anyway. At some gut level, relativists still they think they know right from wrong; if you doubt this, watch them lecture their kids or, better yet, criticize their colleagues.

That said, I am not going to spend time discussing what the concepts of right and wrong really mean, whether they come from God, or whether we always have compelling reasons to act in a moral way. I will not consider meta-ethics, the study of the underlying nature of ethical judgments. Instead, I will simply assume that right and wrong are concepts which make fundamental sense. Even if you don't subscribe to this view, you may be able to slot many of my arguments into your favored alternative moral stance.

In concrete cases, it is often very difficult to discern which particular course of action is right and which is wrong. The skeptic is underappreciated, especially in an age of polarized politics when each side is convinced it is right and the other is unacceptably wrong. Science is our main path to knowledge, and yet so often science tells us that we don't know. That is all the more true for social science, and macroeconomics may well stand at the summit of our epistemic limitations. So, as we consider the realm of politics, we should not engage in the sport of building a coalition of like-minded individuals, defeating competing coalitions, and then implementing as law that which we already know to be best. That's a popular approach, and it makes us feel good about ourselves and our own supposed superiority, but it is unjustified. We need to be more modest when it comes to what we can possibly know.

Philosophers David Hume and William James both understood the smallness of the individual human mind compared to the vast expanse of nature and society, and they emphasized the irrationalities of the human mind when facing the daily problems put before us. If we are building principles for politics, we need approaches which are relatively fortified against human error and the rampant human tendency for self-deception, and which can transcend our own tendencies for excessive "us vs. them" thinking.

Yet at the same time, we need doctrines we can actually believe in and which provide a foundation for a political and social order. A fine-tuned philosophical doctrine which no one accepts or ever could accept won't be of much use. Reconciling the need to accommodate both skepticism and belief is one of the trickiest tasks for any philosophy. If we are indeed skeptics of a sort, how can we believe in anything of real import? To frame this question another way: what should be the roles of reason and of faith as we move forward?

Next, I hold **pluralism** as a core moral intuition. What's good about an individual human life can't be boiled down to any single value. It's not all about beauty or all about justice or all about happiness. Pluralist theories are more plausible, postulating a variety of relevant values, including human well-being, justice, fairness, beauty, the artistic peaks of human achievement, the quality of mercy, and the many different and, indeed, sometimes contrasting kinds of happiness. Life is complicated! That means no single value is a trump card which overwhelms all other values in all instances, and thus there is a fundamental messiness to the nature of the good. A recognition of this messiness may at first seem inconsistent with an attachment to rigid ideals of prosperity and liberty; that reconciliation will be a central issue in this book.

Sometimes my fellow economists argue that "satisfying people's preferences" is the only value that matters, because in their view it encapsulates all other relevant values. But that approach doesn't work. It is not sufficiently pluralistic, as it also matters whether our overall society encompasses standards of justice, beauty, and other values from the plural canon. "What we want" does not suffice to define the good. Furthermore, we must often judge people's preferences by invoking other values external to those preferences. To give an extreme example, when we condemn a man who beats his wife, must we really calculate whether the suffering of the victim exceeds the pleasure of the hitter? I think not. Furthermore, if individuals are poorly informed, confused, or downright inconsistent—as nearly all of us are, at times—the notion of "what we want" isn't always so clear. So while I am an economist, and I will use a lot of economic arguments, I won't always side with the normative approach of my discipline, which puts too much emphasis on satisfying preferences at the expense of other ethical values. We need to make more room for justice and beauty.

I sometimes call myself a "two-thirds utilitarian," since I look first to human well-being when analyzing policy choices. If a policy harms human well-being, on net, it has a high hurdle to overcome. If "doing the right thing" does not create a better world in terms of well-being on a repeated basis, we should begin to wonder whether our conception of "the right thing" makes sense. That said, human well-being is not always an absolute priority—thus the half-in-jest reference to my two-thirds weighting for utility. We sometimes ought to do that which is truly just, even if it is painful for many people. I should not forcibly excise one of your kidneys simply because you can do without it and someone else needs one. We should not end civilization to do what is just, but justice does sometimes trump utility. And justice cannot be reduced to what makes us happy or to what satisfies our preferences.[1]

In short, my philosophical starting points are:

1. Smart and Williams (1973), Scheffler (1982), and Singer (1993) offer some standard treatments of consequentialism, the evaluation of choices in terms of their consequences, a philosophical doctrine that includes utilitarianism as one variant. Pettit (1997) offers a good introduction to consequentialist reasoning and why it is persuasive.

1. "Right" and "wrong" are very real concepts which should possess great force.
2. We should be skeptical about the powers of the individual human mind.
3. Human life is complex and offers many different goods, not just one value that trumps all others.

With this in mind, let's now turn to the question of choice. When it comes to choice, I see some key questions for the individual as well as the collective. Why do we prefer one choice over another? To what extent do we have good reasons for such preferences? Exactly which choices should we make?

To make progress on these queries, I will consider six critical issues, each of which can help us resolve clashes of value:

1. **Time**

    How should we weight the interests of the present against the more distant future? This relates to a more metaphysical question: do we have legitimate reasons to weight the present more heavily simply because it is the here and now? Does the economic approach to time discounting—which suggests that the future declines in moral importance as it becomes more distant in time, and in rough proportion to market interest rates—apply? (I say no.) This is a key question to consider when deciding how much we should commit to making our future world a better place.

2. **Aggregation**

    Aggregation refers to how we resolve disagreements and how we decide that the wishes of one individual should take precedence over the wishes of another. Here's a very simple example: if your daughter wants to watch Japanese anime on television and your son wants to watch a Disney cartoon, whose desire should prevail? If John desires greater income equality and

Cecilia does not, on what grounds might we elevate one preference over another?

There are well-known responses these quandaries in economics, for instance the Arrow and Sen impossibility theorems, which suggest that aggregation problems are very difficult to solve and are perhaps altogether intractable. Some commentators read these theorems as evidence that we cannot rationally decide who should get his or her way when people disagree. Yet we must resolve issues of clashing preferences virtually every day of our lives, so we cannot in fact retreat into a kind of operative nihilism. I'll tip my hand and say that I am optimistic that this problem can be resolved.

3. Rules

The notion that rules and general principles can govern our choices and also our politics is a compelling one. But what does it mean to adhere to such rules and principles? We'd like to think that rules have independent power and intrinsic force, but that view is difficult to defend under fire. After all, virtually all rules have exceptions. Sometimes it is moral to lie in order to save innocent victims from their persecutors, to cite one classic example from moral philosophy. When we decide whether and when to break a given rule, we're back to judging individual cases, which is what rules were supposed to get us away from in the first place.

Philosophers pose similar questions in a different language. They debate the doctrine of rule utilitarianism, which suggests that we should choose those rules that maximize social utility. Similarly, a broader and more pluralist approach called rule consequentialism looks for the rules that will maximize a broader definition of good consequences.[2] But does the doctrine of rule utilitarianism (or rule consequentialism) collapse into act utili-

---

2. For two recent discussions of what consequentialism means, see Hurley (2009) and Brown (2011).

tarianism? That is, are we not always second-guessing our adherence to the supposed rule? Are we morally justified in breaking a rule when the individual circumstances dictate we should?

Under one common view, rules are a mere fiction, a phony trick—albeit a useful one—that holds no independent force in our moral reckoning. Can we generate a coherent morality in which we respect rules and principles for their own sake? Can we make a fundamental choice to think in terms of rules and principles per se? Might we even obsess over rules? Or will we find ourselves caught in the trap of always worrying about the exceptions, thus ending up right back where we started, with rules as a useful fiction?

I'm going to speak up for rules.

4.   Radical uncertainty

I'm a skeptic, sure, but I'm a skeptic with a can-do temperament who realizes how paralyzing skepticism can be. It is, of course, extraordinarily difficult to predict the distant future. I'm not just talking about the difficulty of constructing good theories in the social sciences and then testing those theories against the data; we also have to contend with our broader inability to trace definitive chains of cause and effect in human affairs.

I'm still bugged by some pretty common problems from science fiction and speculative fiction. Here's an example: even our tiniest actions can theoretically set off a chain reaction with far-reaching repercussions. Imagine if Hitler's father—or how about Caesar's father?—had arrived one second later to the marriage bed. A different sperm and egg would have come together, and the entire course of human history might have been radically different. When I was a kid, I read a comic book story about a team of researchers who went back in time to observe the dinosaurs. By mistake, their ship crushes a single leaf, and all of human history is changed; in this alternate reality, the American Indians end up conquering Europe. If there is a future version of Hitler, my writing this book—and your reading it—may well play a role in his later conception and birth. Who knows?

Given such long-run uncertainty, how can we possibly pretend to assess the good and bad consequences of our actions? How can we make any decision at all without succumbing to moral paralysis and total uncertainty?

Usually, people skirt past this problem by saying we must simply do the best we can. There is much truth to that, but the question remains: how can we use our epistemic modesty to make better choices?

5.   **How can we believe in rights?**

The notion of intrinsic human rights comes up often in philosophic discussion, and it exercises considerable sway in the world more broadly, including in international law. But within philosophical circles, the foundations upon which the concept of rights rest are often viewed as shaky. Even when a notion of intrinsic rights is accepted, they are still seen as relying too much on pure intuition. I'm not going to argue my own understanding of rights from scratch, but I do believe in (nearly) absolute human rights. I will put forward a doctrine of "rights without embarrassment." That may not be nearly as strong as absolute proof of intrinsic rights, but some key elements of ethical reasoning do support the notion of objectively valid human rights, and, indeed, of their nearly sacred character.[3]

As you might expect of someone who speaks up for rules, I'm going to speak up for rights, too.

---

3. For one recent look at rights, which also surveys many of the major questions I address here, see Griffin (2008). Wenar (2013) also surveys some aspects of the current debate, in addition to his original contributions. On intuitionism, see Huemer (2005).

6. Common sense morality

Common sense morality holds that we should work hard, take care of our families, and live virtuous but self-centered lives, while giving to charity as we are able and helping out others on a periodic basis. Utilitarian philosophy, on the other hand, appears to suggest an extreme degree of self-sacrifice. Why should a mother tend to her baby when she could sell it and use the profits to save a greater number of babies in Haiti? Shouldn't anyone with medical training be obliged to move to sub-Saharan Africa to save the maximum number of lives? What percentage of your income do you give to charity? Given the existence of extreme poverty, shouldn't it be at least fifty percent? Is eating that ice cream cone really so important? Common sense morality implies it's OK to enjoy that chocolate, but utilitarianism says otherwise.

British philosopher Henry Sidgwick was obsessed with figuring out whether the recommendations of utilitarianism and common sense morality could be made broadly compatible; later, British philosopher Derek Parfit picked up on the same theme. And if those two approaches are not compatible, which ethical perspective should we prefer, and why?

The six issues listed above all involve some tough questions. Yet I will put forward and defend a controversial claim: that all of these difficult problems are more of a piece than we might think. These problems can indeed be resolved, and with a relatively small number of intellectual and philosophical "moves." By no means will these moves make life easy for normative evaluation; instead, they will create new problems. But I will suggest that we trade in our old problems for these new ones. In fact, I will suggest that, upon reasoned examination, we *must* trade in our old problems for these new ones.

The fundamental philosophical moves I have in mind are twofold:

First, I do not take the productive powers of economies for granted. Production could be much greater than it is today, and our lives could be more splendid. Or, if we make some big mistakes, production could be much lower, and we could all be much poorer. This simple observation allows us to put the idea of production at the center of our moral theory, because without production, value is problematic. For all of her failings, Ayn Rand is the one writer who has best understood the importance of production to moral theory—a point she expressed enthusiastically and at great length, albeit with numerous unfortunate caricatures. It is the work of capital, labor, and natural resources, driven by the creative individual mind, which undergird the achievements of our civilization. Whether or not you agree with all of Rand's political views, she is correct in her stance that we must not take the existence of wealth for granted.

Second, I will seek to revise some of our intuitive assumptions about moral distance. Which individuals should exert more of an influence over our choices, and which should exert less? I will argue, for instance, that the individuals who will live in the future should be less distant from us, in moral terms, than many people currently believe. Their interests should hold greater sway over our calculations, and that means we should invest more in the future. Even though it is sometimes hard for us to imagine how our actions will affect future people, especially those from the more distant future, their moral import remains high. I will therefore be asking humans to have greater faith in the future. I am not asking for faith at the expense of reason, but it will nonetheless require an attitude very much akin to faith to consistently think so far ahead in our calculations. It is no accident that religious people often have higher rates of fertility, or that they engage in so many long-term business and charitable projects, as Max Weber observed long ago.

As I consider the questions outlined above, I will focus on clashing arguments and the substantive bottom line. I do not devote much time to building consensus on familiar material, surveying what everyone has said on a particular topic, or other such niceties. I do not retread familiar ground and then offer tentative suggestions for tackling these tough problems at the very end. I do not argue by elimination by focusing on the weaknesses of other views and downplaying the weaknesses of my own. Instead, I seek to start with the tough questions, pinpoint the hardest points of dispute, and spend the rest of my time trying to pick up the pieces. That is what I like to read, and therefore it is what I'm trying to write.

This is where my internal debate stands. I hope you enjoy it. If you are the kind of reader I want, you will feel I have not pushed hard enough on the tough questions, no matter how hard I push.

I also hope that you will respond by taking a stronger stand on behalf of the ideals of freedom and prosperity. I hope you will join more firmly in the cause of making our civilization stronger, more durable, and more wondrous. In this book, I suggest that we need a radical reawakening. And this reawakening will prove to be a new and compelling way of reaffirming our own power as individuals.

With that in mind, let's proceed.

Where does value come from? How is value created and maintained and augmented over time? These simple questions sound like clichés, but they are central to ethics.

Let's consider the idea of systems, networks, norms, or policies which create systematically increasing value over time, without apparent end. Milton Friedman used to argue that there is no such thing as a free lunch, but at some level this has to be false. The universe exists—who had to pay for it? (Moreover, some cosmological hypotheses hold that the universe arose out of quantum fluctuations and is forever giving rise to offshoots, baby universes, all "for free.") This seems to suggest that there has been at least one free lunch—a big one—in our history, so maybe there are others. So, what can we usefully think of as a free lunch when it comes to social decision-making? After all, planet Earth somehow evolved from a bunch of trilobites to trillions of dollars in GDP and a Louvre full of paintings.

Since free lunches aren't always easy to find, we should think about where free lunches might be hiding and why some of those free lunches might be less than evident. In particular, we might uncover hidden gains if we more closely consider the dimension of time. Maybe some of our choices release a steady stream of benefits, but we don't see them as clearly as we ought to. As Adam Smith noted in the eighteenth century, we tend to visualize future events very poorly and with a deficit of proper imagination.

In economics, there is at least one (hypothetical) example of a free lunch. Economist Frank Knight wrote of the Crusonia plant, a mythical, automatically growing crop which generates more output each period. If you lay the seeds, the plant just grows; you don't have to water it or tend to it. Imagine, for example, an apple tree that yields several apples each year. The tree also produces apple seeds. The apple seeds germinate, resulting in a steady and indeed growing supply of new apples and also of new apple trees, albeit based on some measure of sun and rain. A Crusonia plant, measured in terms of its ability to produce apples, might grow five percent each year on net. At the same time, it looks like a modest apple tree and does not appear to resolve any key ethical or political questions.

The idea of the Crusonia plant may sound unrealistic or a bit silly, but it's a useful example for pinpointing the nature of our quest. The Crusonia plant is an example of a free lunch—at least a free lunch of apples—once you have obtained it. (By the way, if you're wondering why it's called the Crusonia plant, it's named after Robinson Crusoe's island; in the Daniel Defoe novel, Crusonia was littered with trees that yielded fruit for nothing, requiring no labor or effort from Crusoe or anyone else. Thus Crusoe enjoyed some free lunches of his own.)

Frank Knight postulated the Crusonia plant in order to make some technical points about the theory of capital and investment, but those debates have since passed. In contrast, I see the Crusonia plant as an entry point for resolving aggregation problems. A Crusonia plant would be more desirable than a plant that dies after a month and leaves no successors, even if this short-lived plant were quite lovely or brilliant. We could compare the two plants in terms of various qualities, such as their color or their scent, but after a while the unceasing free yield of the Crusonia plant has to prove the better choice. At some point the sheer accretion of value from the ongoing growth of the Crusonia plant dominates the comparison. We thus have a principle of both ethics and prudence: when in doubt, choose the Crusonia plant.

When it comes to making tough decisions, we should try to identify which elements in the choice set resemble a Crusonia plant. If we can identify certain choices or policies that give rise to the equivalent of the Crusonia plant's unceasing yield, namely ongoing and self-sustaining surges in value, the case for those choices would be compelling. Furthermore, if it turned out that Crusonia plants were more common than we first thought, aggregation problems would be eased more generally.

So, in a social setting, what might count as analogous to a Crusonia plant? Look for social processes which are ongoing, self-sustaining, and which create rising value over time. The natural candidate for such a process is economic growth, or some modified version of that concept. If sustainably positive-sum institutions exist, there may be Crusonia plants all over the place. As we'll see, standard definitions of economic growth do not fully qualify as true Crusonia plants, in part because they ignore environmental sustainability and in part because they do not adequately value leisure time. Nevertheless, if we think about economic growth a little more broadly, we will have a relevant Crusonia plant on which to base our decisions.

Economists use the concept of gross domestic product (GDP) to refer to the total value of goods and services produced over some period of time, usually a year or a quarter. The rate of economic growth is the rate at which GDP increases. I will use the concept somewhat differently, postulating that GDP should properly be measured in terms of maximizing the long-term rate of economic growth. This is not how GDP is currently measured by most governments. "Wealth Plus," if I may use that term to refer to the accumulated gains from growth, accounts for leisure time, household production (valuable activities you perform at home for free, be it mending socks or using Facebook), and environmental amenities, among other adjustments. Current GDP statistics have a bias toward what can be measured easily and relatively precisely, rather than focusing on what contributes to human welfare.

With that in mind, I will define the concept of Wealth Plus as follows:

Wealth Plus: The total amount of value produced over a certain time period. This includes the traditional measures of economic value found in GDP statistics, but also includes measures of leisure time, household production, and environmental amenities, as summed up in a relevant measure of wealth.

In this context, maximizing Wealth Plus does not mean that everyone should work as much as possible. A fourteen-hour work day might maximize measured GDP in the short run, but it would be less propitious over time once we take into account the value of leisure, not to mention the potential for burnout. Still, this standard is going to value a strong work ethic.[1]

Maximizing Wealth Plus also does not mean destroying the natural environment. It's now well understood that environmental problems can lower or destroy economic growth through feedback effects. We should therefore protect the environment enough to preserve and indeed extend economic growth into the more distant future.

More broadly, the principle of Wealth Plus holds that we should maintain higher growth over time, and not just for a single year or for some other, shorter period of time. Maximizing the sustainable rate of economic growth does not mean pursuing immediate growth at the expense of all other values. Policies that prioritize growth at breakneck speed are frequently unstable, both economically and politically. The Shah of Iran, for instance, tried to bring his country into the modern age very rapidly. Growth rates were high for a while but in the longer run could not be maintained. Since the Iranian Revolution, Iran's economy has backslid. The Shah's forced modernization did not maximize true economic growth, and more cautious policies likely would have been better and more sustainable.[2]

---

1. In terms of providing operational guidance in calculating Wealth Plus, the two best efforts I know of are Jones and Klenow (2016) and Becker, Philipson, and Soares (2005). For a good piece that puts production and productivity at the center of moral theory, see Stanczyk (2012), and also works by the philosopher David Schmidtz.

2. For a formal look at the concept of sustainability, see Heal (1998).

The concept of sustainability, as embedded within the Crusonia plant idea, thus focuses our attention on the prerequisites for a durable civilization. And although many people currently live in relative peace and prosperity, we should not take its durability for granted. If we look at the broader historical record, economic growth is hardly the rule, and civilizations are fragile. Michael Shermer has compiled an informal database on civilizational survival that catalogues sixty civilizations, including Sumeria, Mesopotamia, Babylonia, the eight dynasties of Egypt, six civilizations in Greece, the Roman Republic and Empire, various dynasties and republics of China, four periods in Africa, three in India, two in Japan, six in Central and South America, and six in modern Europe and America. He finds that the average civilization endured for 402.6 years. He also finds that decline comes more rapidly over time; since the collapse of the Roman Empire, the average duration of a civilization has been only 304.5 years.[3]

While the exact numerical estimates depend on how we define the concept of civilization and how we pin down start and end points, the more general point about the fragility of civilizations stands. Human beings can and indeed do experience significant and ongoing losses of their prosperity and freedom.[4]

3. See Shermer (2002). Rees (2003) and especially Posner (2004) both focus on issues of civilizational collapse. S.E. Finer (1999, 30–34) provides an alternative look at civilizational survival, under the heading "Total Life-Spans." He defines a civilization in broader terms than does Shermer, so for him ancient Egypt is one civilization, not eight. Civilizations have correspondingly longer life spans. Some of the longer-lived civilizations include Egypt (2,820 years), China (2,133 years), and the Byzantine Empire (1,962 years). The Venetian Republic lasted 1,112 years. The shorter examples include the Achaemenid Persian Empire (220 years) and the Sassanian Persian Empire (427 years). Finer also develops the more finely grained category of civilizational breakdowns, which occur more frequently. A breakdown is the "disintegration of a previously united state" (32), in contrast to the more severe examples of total civilizational collapse. Egyptian breakdowns occur after periods of 675, 184, 206, 215, and 1,238 years. Chinese breakdowns occur after periods of 400, 500, 442, 360, 326, 69, and 936 years. Assyrian breakdowns occur after periods of 157, 82, 38, 143, and 312 years. Arnold Toynbee, in his classic *A Study of History*, classifies world history into twenty-six civilizations. By his count, sixteen of these civilizations no longer exist. Samuel Huntington's *The Clash of Civilizations* (1996, 44–45), citing Matthew Melko (1969), refers to twelve major civilizations, seven of which have perished.

4. Samuel Huntington (1996) cites a variety of definitions of "civilization," including the concepts of "settled, urban, and literate" (40) and "the broadest cultural entity" (43). Fernández–Armesto (2001, 16–20), referring to the work of Kenneth Clark, designates a civilization as a society with the confidence to build for the future. Clark (1969) noted that while he did not know exactly what civilization was, he could recognize it when he saw it. Matthew Melko (1969, 113) remarks that "when a civilization is operating effectively, it is likely to grow."

We might wonder whether we could maximize the relevant pluralist values by existing at a very modest population size and economic level for a very long time—living in harmony with nature, so to speak. Think of Tolkien's quaint hobbits. But poorer societies from the past have collapsed repeatedly through military weakness, ecological catastrophe, famine, tyranny, and natural disasters, among other factors.

Keep in mind that the wealthier tyrant will conquer or at least disrupt the noble savage. Even if in principle the life of the noble savage were best, no society that follows this path can, on its own, keep its autonomy in the longer run. Given the trajectory of human development, some society will always have tanks and nuclear weapons, whether we like it or not. It is also important to note that the more benevolent societies tend to be both richer and more technologically advanced—further evidence of the importance of sustainable economic growth.

Furthermore, primitive warfare appears to have been at least as frequent, as bloody, and as arbitrary in its violence as modern warfare.[5] Earlier societies were neither idyllic nor peaceful. So returning to the past, or attempting to throttle economic growth, does not guarantee the future prospects of a civilization, much less its comfort. In other words, we need to move forward rather than seek a static, quiet existence, yet our path requires a tightrope act, balancing progress and stability along the way.

We can already see that three key questions should be elevated in their political and philosophical importance, namely:

1. What can we do to boost the rate of economic growth?
2. What can we do to make our civilization more stable?
3. How should we deal with environmental problems?

---

5. Diamond (2005) focuses on how ecological catastrophes have destroyed or damaged civilizations of the more distant past. On the brutality of primitive warfare, see Keeley (1996) and LeBlanc (2003).

The first of these is commonly considered a right-wing or libertarian concern, the second a conservative preoccupation, and the third, especially in the United States, is most commonly associated with left-wing perspectives. Yet these questions should be central, rather than peripheral, to every political body. We can see right away how the political spectrum must be reshaped to adequately address these concerns. Politics should be about finding the best means to achieve these ends, rather than disputing the importance of these ends.

How good is growth, anyway?

The history of economic growth indicates that, with some qualifications, growth alleviates misery, improves happiness and opportunity, and lengthens lives. Wealthier societies have better living standards, better medicines, and offer greater personal autonomy, greater fulfillment, and more sources of fun. While measured wealth does not exactly correspond to Wealth Plus, these two concepts have come pretty close to one another in the past, especially across the range of outcomes we have observed (as opposed to hypothetical thought experiments and counterfactuals).

We often forget how overwhelmingly positive the effects of economic growth have been. Economist Russ Roberts reports that he frequently polls journalists about how much economic growth there has been since the year 1900. According to Russ, the typical response is that the standard of living has gone up by around fifty percent. In reality, the U.S. standard of living has increased by a factor of five to seven, estimated conservatively, and possibly much more, depending on how we measure prices and the values of outputs over time, a highly inexact science.

The data show just how much living standards have gone up. In 1900, for instance, almost half of all U.S. households (forty-nine percent) had more than one occupant per room and almost one quarter (twenty-three percent) had over 3.5 persons per sleeping room. Slightly less than one quarter (twenty-four percent) of all U.S. households had running water, eighteen percent had refrigerators, and twelve percent had gas or electric lighting. Today, the figures for all of these stand at ninety-nine percent or higher. Back then, only five percent of households had telephones, and none of them had radio or TV. The high school graduation rate was only about six percent, and most jobs were physically arduous and had high rates of disability or even death. In the mid-nineteenth century, a typical worker might have put in somewhere between 2,800 and 3,300 hours of work a year; that estimate is now closer to 1,400 to 2,000 hours a year.[6]

Until recently, polio, tuberculosis, and typhoid were common ailments, even among the rich. U.S. presidents George Washington, James Monroe, Andrew Jackson, Abraham Lincoln, Ulysses S. Grant, and James A. Garfield all caught malaria during their lives. Antibiotics and vaccines have existed for only a tiny fraction of human history, and it is no coincidence that they emerged in the wealthiest time period humanity has ever seen. There is also a strong and consistent relationship between wealth and rates of infant mortality; small children do best when they are born into wealthier countries, and that is because wealth supplies the resources to take better care of them.

As recently as the end of the nineteenth century, life expectancy in Western Europe was roughly forty years of age, and food took up fifty to seventy-five percent of a typical family budget. The typical diet in eighteenth-century France had about the same energy value as that of Rwanda in 1965, the most malnourished nation for that year. One effect of this deprivation was that most people simply did not have much energy for life.[7]

In earlier time periods, most individuals performed hard physical labor, and a college or university education—or even a high school education—was a luxury. Leisure time has risen with economic growth. In 1880, about four-fifths of individuals' discretionary time was spent

6. These figures are drawn from the U.S. Census Bureau, via an unpublished paper by Bradford DeLong, "Lecture 2: Slow Growth and Poverty in the North Atlantic, 1800–1870." On work hours, see Huberman and Minns (2007).

7. See Fogel (2004, 8, 9, 34).

working, according to economist Robert Fogel. Today we spend about fifty-nine percent of our time doing what we like, and that may rise to seventy-five percent by 2040.[8]

The splendors of the modern world are not just frivolous baubles; they are important sources of human comfort and well-being. Imagine that a time traveler from the eighteenth century were to pay a visit to Bill Gates today. He would find televisions, automobiles, refrigerators, central heating, antibiotics, plentiful food, flush toilets, cell phones, personal computers, and affordable air travel, among other remarkable benefits. The most impressive features of Gates's life, seen from the point of view of a person from the eighteenth century, are those shared by most citizens of wealthy countries today. My smartphone is as good as his. The very existence of an advanced civilization—the product of cumulative economic growth—confers immense benefits to ordinary citizens, including their ability to educate and entertain themselves and choose one life path over another. For further arguments along these lines, I recommend Steven Pinker's recent book, *Enlightenment Now: The Case for Reason, Science, Humanism, and Progress*.[9]

The economic growth of the wealthier countries benefits the very poor as well, though sometimes with considerable lags. The distribution of wealth changes over time, and not all growth trickles down, but as an overall historical average, the bottom quintile of an economy shares in growth.[10] You can see this by comparing the bottom quintile in, say, the United States to the bottom quintile in India or Mexico.

The richer economy can also do more to elevate the living standards of immigrants. Poor people who move to rich countries usually receive higher incomes and have better living conditions, and their children do better still. The richer the receiving country, the more new immigrants tend to benefit. Central American immigrants to the

---

8. See Fogel (2004, 70).

9. I am indebted to Don Boudreaux for this framing of the point.

10. See for instance Dollar and Kraay (2000).

United States do better than Central American immigrants to Mexico or Nepalese immigrants to India. Immigrants also send remittances back home at a rate that far exceeds governmental foreign aid. Actual upward mobility in the United States far exceeds what the usual numbers indicate, because published statistics on upward mobility do not typically include a comparison with pre-immigration outcomes.

But the chain of benefits does not stop there. Migrants will often return to their home countries, bringing new skills and new business connections. Both India and Israel have developed vibrant technology and software scenes precisely because of their close ties with the start-up scene of the United States. English-language universities in English-speaking countries have trained many thousands of Asian students in science and engineering, again leading to new businesses and, eventually, higher economic growth in their home countries.

New medicines and technologies developed in wealthy nations also make their way to the rest of the world, as illustrated most conspicuously by the rapid spread of the cell phone and now the smartphone. One study predicts that if the leading twenty-one industrial countries were to boost their R&D by half a percentage point of GDP, U.S. output alone would grow by fifteen percent. But it doesn't end there: output in Canada and Italy would grow by about twenty-five percent, and the output of all industrial nations would increase by 17.5 percent, on average. In the less economically developed countries, output would increase by about 10.6 percent on average.[11]

Although these historical processes have often embodied unfairness and long lags of decades or more, economic growth has nonetheless brought wealth to the poor and elevated their status. The Greek city-states and the Roman Empire benefited from maritime trade across the Mediterranean; those regions in turn spread growth-enhancing institutions around Europe, Northern Africa, and the Middle East.

11. See Helpman (2004, 84).

The commercial revolution of the late Middle Ages and Renaissance reopened many of the trade routes of antiquity, and eventually human beings started to climb out of the Malthusian trap of very low per capita incomes at subsistence. The wealth of the West helped to enable the export miracles of the East Asian economies. Today, most poor countries seek greater access to wealthier Western and Asian markets, and flourish if they can achieve it.[12]

For all the recent increases in inequality within individual nations, *global* inequality has declined over the last few decades, in large part because of growth in China and India. And the growth in these emerging nations was largely driven by earlier growth in the West and in East Asia. China, for instance, engaged in "catch-up" growth by adopting Western technologies and exporting to the wealthier nations. China has gone from being a quite poor nation to a "middle-income" nation with a sizable middle and upper class.

Although recent media coverage has focused almost exclusively on within-nation magnitudes, recent world history has been an extraordinarily egalitarian time. It is above all else a story about how global economic growth helps the poor. There has been a squeezing of the middle class in the wealthier nations, in part because of increasing global competition. Still, we have seen economic growth, aggregate wealth, and global income equality all rising together over the last twenty-five years. Many citizens in East Asia, South Asia, and Latin America have seen significant gains in their standard of living, and much of this has been a trickle-down effect from the earlier growth of the wealthier countries. Much of Africa is now following suit, bolstered in part by China's demand for raw materials, and also by the spread of modern technologies such as affordable cell phones.[13]

Sometimes extended periods of growth do not confer full or fair benefits to the poor or lower classes, for instance during the early phase of the British Industrial Revolution in the late eighteenth century.

12. Statistical work on trade, investment, and growth cannot always sort out which variables are endogenous. Nonetheless, the available evidence shows definite correlations between openness to trade and growth; see Helpman (2004, 70–71) for a survey.

13. On the decline in global inequality, see for instance Lakner and Milanovic (2014).

Still, the historical record suggests that it was better for Britain to push ahead with economic growth, as this eventually drove the greatest boost in living standards the world has ever seen. To be sure, there were probably better policies which, had they been adopted, would have distributed the benefits of growth more widely (e.g., fewer wars and Poor Law reform and free trade for the British). But even taking misguided policies into account, Britain fared better by pursuing economic growth rather than turning its back on the idea, even though significant real wage gains for the working class often did not arrive until the 1840s.

Nobel Laureate Amartya Sen has promoted the idea of "capabilities" as, if not quite a substitute for economic growth, then an alternative focus. Sen points out that our positive opportunities in life often matter more than the amount of cash in our bank accounts. He also notes that some parts of the world, such as the state of Kerala in India, have relatively good health and education indicators, even though their per capita incomes are relatively low.

Sen's points are well taken, but they do not put a fundamental dent in the relevance of wealth, or, as I am calling it here, Wealth Plus. The significant benefits accrued from capabilities, such as health benefits, are accounted for in Wealth Plus, even if they are not properly represented in current GDP measures. In other words, Kerala is wealthier than some limited statistical measures imply. Wealth and good social outcomes are still strongly correlated on average, and this correlation is stronger over longer time horizons. For instance, if Kerala does not grow much in more narrow economic terms, it is unlikely to look so impressive in its social indicators fifty or one hundred years from now. Even today, Kerala manages as well as it does in large part because so many Keralans take jobs in wealthier countries, especially in the Gulf States, and send money back home. And compared to other Indian states, Kerala has an above-average measure of wealth, as well as above-average consumption expenditures, both of which are accounted for in traditional statistics.[14]

The truth is that economic growth is the only permanent path out of squalor. Economic growth is how the Western world climbed out of the poverty of the year 1000 A.D. or 5000 B.C. It is how much of East Asia became remarkably prosperous. And it is how our living standards will improve in the future. Just as the present appears remarkable from the vantage point of the past, the future, at least provided growth continues, will offer comparable advances, including, perhaps, greater life expectancies, cures for debilitating diseases, and cognitive enhancements. Billions of people will have much better and longer lives. Many features of modern life might someday seem as backward as we now regard the large number of women in earlier centuries who died in childbirth for lack of proper care.

I myself have written of the great stagnation, a slowdown in growth which overtook the Western world starting in about 1973. It would be a failure of imagination, however, to believe that human progress has run its course. The more plausible view is that progress is unevenly bunched, we have been in a slow period as of late, various new developments are percolating, and we should do our best to help them along. Whether we like it or not, economic growth and technological progress do not always arrive at a steady pace.

World history offers various precedents for the idea of a "great transformation" leading to enormous increases in the quality and quantity of human lives. Our ancestors did not foresee the evolution of humans, the agricultural revolution, the "urban revolution" (Sumeria and Mesopotamia, circa 4000 B.C.), or the Industrial Revolution. For that matter, the East Asian revolution in economic growth was not widely anticipated. Each development dramatically changed the human condition over time, and eventually very much for the better. The history of economic growth, to some extent, is the history of

14. See for instance Venkatraman (2009) and Tsai (2006).

working out the consequences of such unforeseen transformations. It is unlikely that we have seen the last of such revolutions, at least provided that civilization manages to stay afloat.

Looking into the more distant future makes the question of the economic growth rate all the more important. For instance, a two percent rate of economic growth, as opposed to a one percent rate, makes only a small difference across the time horizon of a single year. But as time passes, the higher growth rate eventually brings about a very large boost to well-being. To make this concrete, here's an experiment: redo U.S. history, but assume the country's economy had grown one percentage point less each year between 1870 and 1990. In that scenario, the United States of 1990 would be no richer than the Mexico of 1990.[15]

It is also worth pondering some comparisons with higher rates of economic growth, of the sort we often see in emerging economies. At a growth rate of ten percent per annum, as has been common in China, real per capita income doubles about once every seven years. At a much lower growth rate of one percent, such an improvement takes about sixty-nine years.

Robert E. Lucas, Nobel Laureate in Economics, put the point succinctly: "The consequences for human welfare involved in questions like these are staggering: once one starts to think about [exponential growth], it is hard to think about anything else."[16]

Even if you don't regard material wealth as central to human well-being, economic growth brings many other values, including, for instance, much greater access to the arts and education. Economic growth also gives individuals greater autonomy and minimizes the chance that their destiny will be determined by the time and place in

15. Cowen (2004).

16. See Lucas (1988, 5).

which they were born. It remains true that many individuals are born poor or are born into families that do not much respect formal education or are born far away from cities. Still, ask yourself a simple question: has there ever been a time in human history when so many individuals had such a good chance of becoming world-class scientists?

Individuals today are more able to shape their futures, choose their friends, communicate with the outside world, and weave together diverse cultural strands when building out their personal narratives. Benjamin M. Friedman, in his brilliant *The Moral Consequences of Economic Growth*, shows just how many of the virtues of the modern world depend on higher and indeed growing levels of wealth.[17]

The bottom line is this: the more rapidly growing economy will, at some point, bring about much higher levels of human well-being—and other plural values—on a consistent basis. If some set of choices or policies gives us a higher rate of economic growth, those same choices or policies are akin to a Crusonia plant.

Does economic growth make us happier?

Many of us are prone to speculating about where in the world the quality of life is highest and where the people are happiest. Is it in the richest countries? The countries where the people have the best psychological attitudes? Or is there some other answer to this question?

Recent research suggests that wealth boosts happiness and that this holds true for a great variety of people, including for the relatively wealthy, who are already meeting their basic needs. Economists Betsey Stevenson and Justin Wolfers, in the most comprehensive study of the income-happiness link to date, find that the relationship between measured well-being and income is roughly linear-log, which implies that income boosts happiness even at higher levels of earnings. A comprehensive study by Nobel Laureate economist Angus

---

17. See Friedman (2006). On the connection between the arts and economic growth, see Cowen (1998). For a recent defense of GDP maximization, see Oulton (2012). For a recent philosophic defense of the importance of economic growth based on pluralistic considerations, see Moller (2011). Stanczyk (2012) considers the importance of "productive justice," namely making sure the output gets produced in the first place.

Deaton finds similar results, namely that extra income brings extra happiness, even in relatively wealthy settings.[18]

An older body of literature suggests that additional riches do not make citizens in wealthy countries any happier, at least not above a certain level of wealth. The core evidence here is taken from questionnaires that ask people how happy they are. Once a country has a per capita income of somewhat above $10,000 a year or more in current U.S. dollars, the aggregate income-happiness link appears weak to many observers. Some commentators argue that the curve flattens out at about half of current American per capita income. These results cast doubt upon whether economic growth does in fact yield ongoing benefits in terms of happiness.[19]

Despite this evidence, I see wealth and happiness as comoving in the broad sense, again subject to a properly sophisticated understanding of wealth.

The observation of a nearly flat happiness-wealth relationship says more about the nature of language than it does about the nature of happiness. To give an example, if you ask the people of Kenya how happy they are with their health, you'll get a pretty high rate of reported satisfaction, not so different from the rate in the healthier countries, and in fact higher than the reported rate of satisfaction in the United States. The correct conclusion is not that Kenyan hospitals possess hidden virtues or that malaria is absent in Kenya, but rather that Kenyans have recalibrated their use of language to reflect what they can reasonably expect from their daily experiences. In similar fashion, people in less happy situations or less happy societies often attach less ambitious meanings to the claim that they are happy. Evi-

18. See for instance Stevenson and Wolfers (2008, 2013), Sacks, Stevenson, and Wolfers (2010), and Deaton (2007).

19. On the flattening of the curve, see for instance Helliwell (2002, 28). Other relevant sources are Argyle (1999), Oswald (1997), and Myers (2000). Wealthy countries, when they become wealthier over time, do not in general become happier in the aggregate. In some cases (e.g., the United States 1946–1991), greater wealth is correlated with lower levels of self–reported happiness; see Dieter (1984), Blanchflower and Oswald (2000), Diener and Oishi (2000), Myers (2000), Kenny (1999), Lane (1998), Frey and Stutzer (2000), and Easterlin (1995). On the United States, see Frey and Stutzer (2002a, 76–77). For a criticism of the income–happiness link from a time use perspective, see Kahneman et al. (2006).

dence based on questionnaires will therefore underrate the happiness of people in wealthier countries.[20]

The literature on happiness often focuses on aspiration or treadmill effects. Under this view, you get more, but you also start expecting or aspiring to more. Greater wealth therefore translates into less happiness. But it is unlikely that treadmill effects "eat up" all of the happiness gains from greater wealth. Along the lines of the Kenya example, growing wealth also causes people to recalibrate their language and affects how they would respond to questions about their happiness. If happiness itself is subject to framing effects, surely *talk* about happiness is subject to framing effects as well; if anything, it may be easier to recalibrate your language than to recalibrate your expectations of happiness.

The wealthy develop higher standards for when they consider themselves to be "happy" or "very happy." If you are a millionaire living next door to a billionaire, you might be less likely to report that you are ecstatically well-off, even though your day-to-day existence is pretty sweet. The failure to issue a totally glowing report does not mean that you spend all of your time envying the billionaire or suffering because of your lower relative status; you can still lord your wealth over plenty of other people, if you so desire. But the presence of your even wealthier neighbor may indeed cause you to have a higher standard for how you use the terms "happy" or "very happy."

Thus even a constant level of reported happiness implies growth in real happiness over time, because the word "happy" takes on ever more ambitious meanings as society accumulates more wealth and richer experiences. Life improvements do generally make us happier, while both our expectations for happiness and our reporting standards for "being happy"—our use of language—adjust upwards.

20. See Deaton (2007).

The belief that greater wealth correlates with greater happiness is supported by direct observation. Many individuals strive to earn higher incomes, even after they have experienced the strength of aspiration and treadmill effects. It's not that they are all being tricked, but rather that they know at a gut level that money will help them achieve valuable ends or that it will help their families. Individuals value happiness for their families as well as for themselves, even if this particular channel of happiness is quite indirect and is not always reflected in their daily moods or their moment-to-moment self-reports.

It is also the case that within a country, wealthier people report unambiguously higher levels of happiness, on average, than do poorer people.[21] For all the talk about how some happiness studies present a revisionist view of material wealth, this result has not been challenged, and it pretty decisively demonstrates that, at least on average, wealth brings more happiness. To some extent, the greater self-reported happiness of the wealthy may reflect a zero-sum relative status effect, namely that the wealthier people feel better, but their possessions make the poor feel worse off. Nonetheless, it is unlikely that all of the gains from wealth, or even most of the gains, dissipate in zero-sum games. Wealthier lives are easier and happier in absolute terms in numerous ways, as discussed above, and as evidenced by a quick look at where most immigrants wish to migrate, namely to the wealthier countries.

If a wealthy man buys a Mercedes, his neighbor may express greater dissatisfaction with his Volkswagen. That same neighbor, if he had a Lada in Leningrad circa 1976, might express a high or at least decent level of satisfaction on a happiness questionnaire. In absolute terms, however, he is still much better off having the Volkswagen in contemporary America than the Lada in 1970s Leningrad. The Volkswagen is a pretty good car, and the Lada broke down a lot and was hard to start. So while the neighbor might envy the wealthy man's Mercedes,

21. See for instance Dieter (1984), among many other sources.

the happiness gains from wealth (and from better cars) do not dissi-pate through envy. Better cars really do make us better off. To put it another way: it is better to envy your neighbor's Mercedes than to envy his horse and buggy. Envying his supersonic transport would be better still.

On top of all of these considerations, happiness isn't a single, simple variable which can be measured unambiguously. Happiness means a lot of different things to different people. Some people may seek temporary stimulations while others may want to feel fulfilled at the end of their lives, and others may seek to maximize the quality of their typical day. Some will seek happiness through the process of out-competing their peers for status, while others will look inward for contemplative delights. Most likely we seek some mix of these ends, but with varying emphases and weights. Wealthier societies offer greater opportunities and freedoms to pursue preferred concepts of happiness, even if this privilege does not always show up in the mea-surement of a single, aggregate number.

The happiness literature takes a relatively limited view of human well-being. Usually the contemporary empirical literature on happi-ness starts with the operational definition of whether an honest, self-aware person would report himself or herself as being happy, if asked. Even if this accurately captures one notion of happiness, and perhaps it does, it is only one component of human well-being. A wealthier economy will offer greater options for structuring choices of work vs. friends, thrills vs. long-term satisfaction, enjoying children vs. a life of theater and travel, and so on.

A wealthier economy also gives us more "fleeting" experiences of happiness. An individual will admit to being happier if he has recent-ly found a dime, or if his soccer team won a big game. These sources of happiness will likely be more frequent and more consistent in the wealthier society. A diverse commercial economy offers more sources of temporary stimulation and more short-term turns of good fortune. This means more new gadgets, more entertaining videos, and more serendipitous encounters with interesting new people. That sounds a bit superficial, and indeed it is, but it is yet another reason why economic growth will boost happiness in its more complex and plural forms.[22]

At most, the happiness literature shows that many changes in individual conditions are irrelevant for our well-being, due to habituation and expectation effects. This conclusion would not, however, eliminate the major benefits of economic growth. Even if many small changes in income are irrelevant or nearly irrelevant to happiness, sufficiently large changes in life circumstances may still boost or harm our welfare.

As an example of how large changes matter, most life catastrophes create significant misery. Very sick individuals have less autonomy, experience more pain, and face the stress of dealing with their condition. The death of a child or close family member profoundly damages happiness for most individuals, and these effects can persist for many years. Torture, extreme stress, rape, and severe physical pain also produce depression, trauma, and persistent unhappiness. Individuals who have been through wars, revolutions, and collapses of civil order very often experience recurring flashbacks, nightmares, irritability, depression, alcoholism, troubled relationships, and an inability to concentrate. However psychologically troubled our modern, wealthy societies may seem, poverty is not the solution to these problems, and in fact it makes them worse.[23]

Some commentators have doubted whether even extreme catastrophes make people less well-off. For instance, the onset of a severe disability or physical handicap may cause individuals to alter their ex-

---

22. See Schwarz and Strack (1999) on some of these dilemmas. Levinson (2013) offers some interesting observations on the role that projection (assuming excess permanence of current events) may play in these evaluations.

23. On the link between catastrophes and unhappiness, see Dyregrov (1990), Lehman et al. (1987), Weiss (1987), Frederick and Loewenstein (1999), Lehman, Wortman, and Williams (1987), Archer (2001), and Wortman et al. (1992). For evidence on the difficulty of recovering from rape, see Meyer and Taylor (1986) and Wirtz and Harrell (1987).

pectations for what their lives will be like. Some or even all of their initial levels of happiness may be reattained by lowering their aspirations, and for that reason the loss in happiness may be blunted. Nonetheless, victims of catastrophes still report lower levels of happiness than do comparable healthy individuals, and many of these victims endure years of significant suffering. Coping mechanisms appear to work the least well when an individual's condition is worsening steadily over time.[24]

So, to the extent that a poorer society results in an ongoing worsening of conditions for many individuals, the associated human suffering will be greater, and this does indeed represent a true loss of human well-being. Once again, there are significant benefits to ongoing and sustainable economic growth.

Extra wealth also serves as a cushion against very bad events, or at least against later declines in wealth. Ten or fifteen years ago, it was common to hear the claim that once a nation reaches the level of material wealth found in Greece, happiness more or less flatlines. Indeed, this was more or less where the flatlining point seemed to be. Yet since the Greek economic crisis, dating from 2009, no one uses the Greek example to make a point about the flatlining of the happiness-income relationship. The country lost almost a quarter of its economic output, unemployment has risen to over twenty percent, there have been riots in the streets, a neo-Nazi party was elected to the legislature, and at times basic medicines have been unavailable. Having some additional reserves of wealth prior to the crisis would have helped the country a good deal, and might have prevented the troubles altogether by easing debt repayment.

Finally, even if we accept the "flatline" empirical result on happiness and wealth, these self-reported happiness questionnaires are given to individuals in normal life circumstances. The answers will not pick up the ability of wealthier economies to postpone or mitigate ex-

---

24. On coping, see Brickman, Coates, and Janoff-Bulman (1978), Bulman and Wortman (1977), Kessler, Price, and Wortman (1985), and Wortman and Silver (1987). On the "core of distress" idea, see Frey and Stutzer (2002a, 56), Wirtz and Harrell (1987), and Stroebe et al. (2001). On once-and-for-all changes vs. ongoing deteriorations, see Frederick and Loewenstein (1999).

treme tragedies. For instance, happiness measures cannot pick up the benefits of greater life expectancy. The dead and incapacitated cannot complain about their situation from the grave, at least not on questionnaires. Life expectancy rises with wealth, but self-reports of happiness miss this benefit because researchers do not poll the dead. If an immigrant, or a child of immigrants, fills out a happiness questionnaire, no comparison is made between their current and pre-immigration state of affairs, either as it was or as it might have been. By design, happiness research draws upon a fixed pool of people living under relatively normal circumstances. This will limit its ability to measure some of the largest benefits brought about by economic growth. If we want to be around to even have the option of answering happiness questionnaires, wealth is extremely important.

The overwhelming benefits of economic growth help us resolve clashing preferences, and thus we are able to overcome what I have called aggregation problems. A higher rate of economic growth, of course, will not make everyone better off; some individuals living today might be better off with more consumption and less work, and thus in a regime with lower rates of economic growth. And even if economic growth makes many people better off in the longer run, it is unlikely to make each and every person better off along the way.

But still, consider how the problem of clashing preferences has been transformed. When rates of economic growth are sustainably higher, there is an overwhelming preponderance of benefits on one side of the scale.

Consider a one percentage point boost to the growth rate, starting at parity. We would need a time horizon of 110.4 years to establish a 3:1 ratio of one GDP (throughout, adjusted for leisure time and sustainability) to another. If we consider a two percentage point boost in the growth rate, we would need a time horizon of 55.5 years. For a more ambitious boost of five percentage points to the growth rate, the time horizon must stretch for only 22.5 years to obtain that 3:1 ratio.

Keep in mind that the indicated number of years expresses when a 3:1 ratio will be reached, comparing a higher to a lower growth rate. Over time, if the higher growth continues, that 3:1 ratio will be exceeded on an ongoing basis and that gap will increase continually. For growth boosts of one, two, and five percentage points net, we would need 161, 81, and 33 years, respectively, to reach a *quintupling* of GDP. So the 3:1 requirement is only a temporary milestone on the path toward even greater discrepancies of wealth and (most likely) well-being.

Economists sometimes argue that a construct known as Arrow's impossibility theorem makes it impossible to resolve clashes of preference. But once we consider happiness and well-being as relevant features for comparing one choice to another, Arrow's impossibility theorem does not hold. Arrow's original theorem assumes, and has to assume, that "happiness talk" (e.g., cardinal, interpersonal utility information) is absent from the comparisons of social states. Think of Arrow's theorem as looking only at the kind of information which can be reflected in observed votes or ordinal rankings. Once a richer information set is introduced, the standard impossibility theorems fade away, and that is why I do not pay them much heed. They were only a big problem in some rather limited theoretical frameworks, and they were never a big problem in the real world in the first place.[1]

The main point is simply that if the gains to the future are significant and ongoing, those gains should eventually outweigh one-time costs by a significant degree, and they will likely carry along other plural values as well.

1. See for instance Sen (1984). As an aside, consider how traditional cost–benefit analysis invokes a "potential compensation" principle to assess the relative importance of policy winners and policy losers. In this traditional economic approach, the key question is whether the gainers' gains exceed the losers' losses, or, in other words, whether the winners could in principle compensate the losers, as measured in material wealth. If so, then cost–benefit analysis recommends the policy, because in principle it could be transformed into a situation where everyone benefits. This is not commonly considered an interpersonal utility comparison, but in practice it functions as one. In most real-world cases, the compensation is never paid from the winners to the losers or even seriously contemplated. So we are judging one set of gains as socially "worth more" than a set of losses on the other side of the scale, and very often the margins of net gain are relatively slender. Note, by the way, that the grossness of the real income comparisons will limit the scope for outcome intransitivity and Scitovsky double-switching problems, as outlined by Chipman and Moore (1978).

Think about South Korea today vs. sub-Saharan Africa. As argued above, a sustainable increase in economic growth, properly understood, will boost many plural values in the medium and long runs. To be sure, some people will be worse off, and some values, in the short to medium run, will not be favored. In these respects, aggregation problems do not disappear. Nonetheless, the competing options do not generally offer a deadlock of roughly equivalent values and interests on each side of the scale, with one side looking better by some moderate amount. South Korea is much better off than, say, the Democratic Republic of Congo by a considerable margin. The higher growth alternative will eventually offer a clear and ongoing preponderance of plural values in its favor, whether it be living standards, women's rights, freedom of choice, the fight against poverty, or other important values. So why not choose that option and recognize that we have rational grounds for preferring it?[2]

This approach to the aggregation problem coincides with common sense morality. Not everyone can be happy about everything all of the time, but we should nonetheless choose the option that makes a strong preponderance of people much better off. Most important plural values will come along for the ride.

Choosing the pro-growth policy addresses some outstanding problems in ethics. For instance, in traditional economics—at least prior to the behavioral revolution and the integration with psychology—it was commonly assumed that what an individual chooses, or would choose, is a good indicator of his or her welfare. But individual preferences do not always reflect individual interests very well. Preferences as expressed in the marketplace often appear irrational, intransitive, spiteful, or otherwise morally dubious, as evidenced by a wide range of vices, from cravings for refined sugar to pornography to grossly actuarially unfair lottery tickets. Given these human imperfections, why should the concept of satisfying preferences be so important? Even if you are willing to rationalize or otherwise defend some of

2. Ronald Dworkin (1980) presents a philosophical critique of the potential compensation principle. He argues that wealth cannot be an end in itself and that we should pay more direct attention to whatever it is we think wealth is proxying for.

these choices, in many cases it seems obvious that satisfying preferences does not make people happier and does not make the world a
better place.

Focusing on the long-term benefits of growth sidesteps such dilemmas. A fast-food cheeseburger is not actually worth $4.89, consider-
ing its potential impact on my future health. The cheeseburger offer is
manipulating my evolutionarily programmed desire for more fat, to
the detriment of my life expectancy. Yet at the same time, living in a
much wealthier society—even one rife with fast food—is still good for
most people, including good for their health. For all the talk about
America's obesity problem, which is indeed real, life expectancy is
still rising with wealth. Indeed, it is wealthy and well-educated people
who are most likely to be thin or to succeed in their diets.

When a higher rate of economic growth is at stake, the relevant comparisons become quite obvious after the passage of enough time. A
given individual is likely better off living an extra five years, receiving
anesthesia at the dentist, enjoying plentiful foodstuffs, having more
years of education, and not losing any children to premature illness.
Similarly, people one hundred years from now will be much better off
if economic growth continues. At some point these cumulative benefits will be sufficiently robust to outweigh particular instances of irrational or misguided preferences. In other words, this approach also
resolves some problems of preference aggregation within the individual self. If part of you wants a cheeseburger and another part of you
wants broccoli, it might be hard to come to a good all-things-consid-
ered judgment of what is best. Is deliciousness more important, or is
your health more important? Yet when we have the opportunity to
opt for a Crusonia plant—higher rates of economic growth—we can
get by with a fairly blunt set of judgments. The wealthier society will,
over time, make just about everyone much better off.

To sum this all up, if we make a broad enough and long enough comparison, we will find that for a lot of choices the aggregation problems are not all that serious, at least not cripplingly so. Given that somewhat cheering reality, I would like to define two principles for practical reasoning. First:

The Principle of Growth: We should maximize the rate of sustainable economic growth, defined in terms of a concept such as Wealth Plus.

The Principle of Growth would return economics to its roots in Adam Smith. Smith held a straightforward, common sense approach to political economy. He understood that the benefits of cumulative growth were significant, especially with the passage of time. It is no accident that his economics treatise was entitled *An Inquiry Into the Nature and Causes of the Wealth of Nations*.

By the way, I see only one episode in human history in which the Principle of Growth was clearly and unambiguously applied, and that is in the East Asian economic miracles, which includes Japan, South Korea, Taiwan, Hong Kong, Singapore, and China (with a caveat for sustainability in the case of China). These histories are normally thought of as big economic successes, and of course they are, but there's more to it than that: they also represent the highest manifestation of the ethical good in human history to date. Whereas Hegel saw the nineteenth-century Prussian state as a manifestation of God's will in history, I am assigning a comparable (but secular) place of importance to the East Asian economic miracles. The word "miracle" truly does apply.

I call the second principle the Principle of Growth Plus Rights:

The Principle of Growth Plus Rights: Inviolable human rights, where applicable, should constrain the quest for higher economic growth.

Bear in mind that I am working with a pluralistic rather than a narrowly utilitarian approach. I will return to the status and nature of such rights later, but for now just think of such rights as binding and absolute. That means: *just don't violate human rights.* If we were willing to trade these rights against a bundle of other plural values, at some sufficiently long time horizon the benefits from higher economic growth would trump the rights in importance, and in essence the rights would cease to be relevant. In other words, the presence of Crusonia plants means that rights—if we are going to believe in them at all—have to be tough and pretty close to absolute in importance if they are to survive as relevant to our comparisons.

Philosopher Robert Nozick wrote of rights as "side constraints." The particular specification of these side constraints need not coincide with Nozick's libertarian vision, and need not coincide with his absolute attachment to all forms of private property or his prohibition of most forms of taxation. Still, these rights will satisfy Nozick's notion of rights as restrictions on the choice set of an individual or an institution. Again, there are some things we just shouldn't do. As I see it, virtually everyone believes in rights of some sort, and thinking in terms of Crusonia plants and aggregation problems helps us identify how those rights fit into moral theory, namely that they have to be pretty strong and nearly absolute.

Note that the traditional notions of "positive rights" or "positive liberties"—both of which refer to people's opportunities—do not fit into this conception of rights. The concept of positive liberties is important, but it is already covered by the imperative to maximize sustainable growth. There is no need to double-count positive liberties, and in fact doing so would be a mistake. The result is that these negative rights, restrictive though they may be, represent a stripped-down set of bare-bones constraints, a series of injunctions about the impermissibility of various forms of murder, torture, and abuse.

That said, I will later argue that we should violate rights to prevent extremely negative outcomes which involve the extinction of value altogether, such as the end of the world, as is sometimes postulated in philosophical thought experiments. If we strip away all of the basic preconditions of moral reasoning and all of the broad empirics behind our judgments and behind our construction of Crusonia plants, sensible notions of rights probably don't apply, or at least their status becomes slippery. In that sense, these postulated rights are not quite absolute, which is why I used the phrase "nearly absolute" earlier. Still, to make this concrete, I have been reading newspapers for over forty years, and I have yet to see an example of a real-world choice that is so far outside the box that I do not wish to apply basic reasoning about rights to it.

Aren't there other exceptions to the rules?

How far does this principle of growth maximization extend? For instance, what if small individual policies affect growth only when considered as a larger collective bundle of growth-enhancing policies? Must we then be agnostic toward the individual policy in that instance? Or can we group those individual policies together in some manner and think in terms of a tighter and more comprehensive set of commitments? And how will this issue relate to rights?

To think through these questions with a transparent example, let's consider one of Derek Parfit's "Mistakes in Moral Mathematics." It goes something like this: if a firing squad of six shooters kills an innocent person, all of them firing accurately at his heart, can we say that any one of the shooters is a murderer? After all, the "marginal product" of any single shooter was zero. Should we punish or invest resources into preventing the actions of any one of the shooters? Does it matter whose bullet arrived first? Should we refuse to prosecute group murders of this kind?

Virtually everyone would agree that participating in such a shooting is wrong. Even though a single additional bullet doesn't change the tragic outcome, if we view that bullet as part of a generalizable rule about how to treat other people—"don't shoot the innocent"—the sum total of rule-following behavior would save the life of the victim. In this case both human rights deontology and a rule consequentialist approach point us in the right direction, namely not firing the additional bullet. Furthermore, the "marginal product alone matters" approach to questions of this nature would induce dire practical consequences. For instance, more and more murders would be carried out by large groups so that no single individual would be liable. Governments obviously don't want to allow this moral or legal loophole, and that is one reason why a rules-based approach to morality is, to some degree, inevitable.[3]

The marksman example is stylized, but it fits many real-world situations. Maybe a single act of corruption has no harmful effects, but corruption in general is harmful, and many corrupt acts will destroy a polity. Would we be justified in condemning a single act of corruption with a fair degree of strictness and severity, without worrying too much about whether the single act of corruption is really going to matter in the long run? A single act of weakness may not damage a person's credibility much, but many weak acts will. A single improvement in procedures may not boost the overall veracity of science very much, but a broader collection of such improvements might make a big difference. Numerous violations of the rule or law may seem harmless enough, but enough of them can be dire once we consider the longer-run expectation and incentive effects. In many of these cases we judge the apparently indifferent individual act in terms of the broader pattern of behavior to which it belongs, and so we can

3. See Parfit (1987, 67) for a related and more complex example. For more recent takes on this dilemma and related problems, see Kagan (2011) and Nefsky (2012), and see Temkin (1996) on a possible role for the Sorites problem.

imagine a moral imperative to try to bring about the larger set of grouped actions.[4]

Some of us might recoil in horror at the notion of a life, or a society, in which everything is governed by strict rules without exceptions. But fear not—rules will not acquire such extreme powers, because most rules are not as important as the growth maximization rule. What makes a growth maximization rule compelling is its attachment to a Crusonia plant, namely very large, ongoing, and indeed compounding gains in human welfare. Some rules, such as "never lie," face embarrassing counterexamples if lying can bring about significant practical benefits in particular instances. But a rule of "maximize the rate of sustainable economic growth" does not face a comparable problem. By definition, *the rule is telling us to follow outcomes with a preponderance of benefits over costs.* So practical costs may overturn or modify some rules, but they will not limit the Principle of Growth, which will be limited only by absolute or near-absolute human rights.

In other words, maximizing sustainable growth as an imperative rule doesn't allow a rule such as "always alphabetize by author rather than by book title" to have comparable moral force, if indeed it has any force at all. Once we move beyond absolute human rights and work toward a Crusonia plant (in this case, sustainable economic growth), most of the remaining morality will be practical in nature, prone to exception, dependent on context, and not exercising much of a tyranny over our lives. It won't necessarily have much to do with rules at all, unless some other perspective, outside of the scope of the arguments at hand, establishes that rules are indeed the proper way to go.[5]

At the end of these arguments, we are led to a surprising conclusion. If the time horizon is sufficiently long, the only non-growth–related values that will bind practical decisions are the absolute side con-

4. On the case for rules, see Brennan and Buchanan (2000), Epstein (1997), and Kydland and Prescott (1977), among many others. Cowen (2011) presents my earlier thoughts. Glazer and Rothenberg (2005) outline how many policy issues involve time consistency issues. See also the literature on rule vs. act utilitarianism, for instance Brandt (1963), Lyons (1965), Regan (1980), Slote (1992), Hooker (2000), Mackie (1985), Scarre (1996), and Feldman (1997). This problem has been present in rule utilitarianism since William Paley in the eighteenth century; see Schneewind (1977, 125-127).

5. An interesting piece on related issues is Väyrynen (2006).

straints, or the inviolable human rights. In other words, *the dual ideals of prosperity and liberty will be central to ethics.* I'll be returning to some arguments for inviolable human rights later, but in the meantime we have a relatively straightforward, exclusive ("worship no other gods"), and practicable formula of "Growth and Human Rights."

I'll now look at the issue of time horizon in more detail. If the proper time horizon for our decisions is quite short, none of these arguments will succeed. I'm going to show why the time horizon matters so much and why we—in most, but not all, cases—should think in terms of very long time horizons.

When I schedule my appointment with the dentist, I wonder whether it should be for this week or the next. Is there anything to be gained or lost from shifting the discomfort from one point in time to another? Is there a justifiable reason for putting off the appointment simply to postpone the discomfort?

So often we are tempted to put pleasure first and postpone our chores and our pains. The present is so real and vivid, and the future seems so distant and abstract. Many people cannot fully grasp that when the future comes, it will be as real as the present is right now.

I am struck by how people respond when they are given a choice between the immediate present, the future, and the more distant future. Very often they are biased toward the immediate present. For instance, a person might realize that a benefit in two years' time is about the same in value as that same benefit in three years' time. That's a rational posture. That same person, however, may prefer a dollar today to three dollars three weeks from now.[1] But when the comparison is between ten years from now and twenty years from now, people exhibit much more patience, and many people would even say that a benefit ten years from now is about as valuable as the same benefit twenty years from now.

In other words, individual time preference usually focuses on the immediate vs. the only somewhat distant. If we can get over our initial

---

1. On that kind of discounting, see Frederick, Loewenstein, and O'Donoghue (2002).

impatience for receiving a reward now, our intellect is very often capable of seeing that we should care about the more distant future as much as we should care about the less distant future. For the most part, we're actually fairly rational about time, except for this fixation on the "now" moment and the "very soon/right away" horizon.

We are programmed for the now moment for reasons which are inapplicable to most of our public policy choices and obsolete as a fundamental tool of moral reasoning. Human beings evolved under brutal hunter-gatherer conditions; they had good reason to pay special attention to the now moment. If you didn't get the "now" right, there might not be a tomorrow. If you let a piece of meat sit, it would spoil or be seized by your neighbor or consumed by marauding animals overnight. It wasn't like sitting on T-Bills in your Fidelity account. So we may have an innate biological preference for the "now," but we will do better if we can get past it, if we can tap into the part of ourselves that recognizes that a benefit in twenty years' time is about as valuable as that same benefit in thirty years' time.

If you are the kind of person who is inclined to seize the current benefit, you will do best if you can find a way to link these immediate rewards to a superior payoff in the future. Young people, uneducated people, and those with lower IQs and problems with cognition or self-control find it hardest to make this connection. Those same people are also more likely to have problems with obesity, gambling, impulse control, and even violence. These correlations don't philosophically prove that their impatient choices are incorrect (maybe the gamblers are the wise ones and the rest of us are fools for missing out on their risky delights), but they do lend support to the idea that these individuals are making a mistake. They are failing to imagine the future and its import. Further evidence suggests that children who are more impatient have more trouble in school and are more likely to encounter disciplinary action.[2]

---

2. Castillo et al. (2011). See also the recent Moffitt et al. (2011) and Mischel, Shoda, and Rodriguez (1989). On the connection between patience and measures of cognitive ability, see Frederick (2005). Ipcher and Zarghamee (2011) consider the connection between positive affect and low time preference.

Very often the choice between the present and the future takes place at the social level. Many social policies influence whether benefits and costs come sooner or later, and if we are to make a choice, we need to decide how impatient we are going to be. I worry about the logical implications of impatience, if we were to apply such impatience to a longer time horizon. Together with Derek Parfit, I once wrote:[3]

> Why should costs and benefits receive less weight, simply because they are further in the future? When the future comes, these benefits and costs will be no less real. Imagine finding out that you, having just reached your twenty-first birthday, must soon die of cancer because one evening Cleopatra wanted an extra helping of dessert. How could this be justified?

Economists and other social scientists often speak of a "discount rate." A discount rate tells us how to compare future benefits to current benefits (or costs) when we make decisions. When the discount rate is high, we are counting future costs and benefits for less. Let's speak in terms of pleasure (or pain) as a magnitude that corresponds, however roughly, to a real number scale. A five percent discount rate, defined annually, means that 100 units worth of pleasure today is equal to 105 units worth of pleasure a year from now. A ten percent discount rate would set this equality at 110 units worth of pleasure a year from now, and so on.

A discount rate of zero means that a future benefit (or cost) counts for as much as a comparable benefit in the present. A person with a zero discount rate would not see any point in putting off going to the dentist. There's no reason not to get it over with.

If there's one thing we've learned, it's that discount rates matter. In your personal life it affects how hard you work, how much you drink and gamble, and what kind of education you get. At the social level,

---

3. Cowen and Parfit (1992, 145).

the discount rate pertains to questions of how hard we should be fighting climate change and how much we should invest in preserving biodiversity. If we dismiss the importance of the distant future, action will not seem imperative. But if we pay heed to the distant future, we will see these as major concerns.

Discounting also matters for how hell-bent we are on pursuing a higher rate of economic growth. A higher growth rate means that the future, at some point in time, will be *much* richer than it would be otherwise, and, as I argued earlier, it also means that human beings will be *much* better off. How compelled should we feel to bring about this wealthier state of affairs? If you only care about today, you won't be as motivated to act in favor of higher sustainable growth.

Most of us are altruistic, especially toward our own children and grandchildren. But this form of partial altruism does not make us care much about other people's grandkids. When people vote or otherwise make choices that affect future generations as a whole, they often behave quite selfishly. Political time horizons tend to be very short, often extending no further than the next election or the next media cycle. Voters are keen to receive more government spending now and postpone the required taxes to the more distant future. Few governments do everything they can to promote economic growth for the more distant future. The bottom line is that caring about the future is not something that happens automatically, even if you dearly love, or will dearly love, your grandchildren. When it comes to the discount rate for social decisions, we need to choose wisely.

For certain decisions, such as whether or not to cut down a tree, market forces induce even selfish people to think about the more distant future. If you leave the tree standing, it might be worth more money. If you own a Rembrandt painting, you'll probably keep it in decent shape, even if you're a selfish, uncultured bastard who doesn't care about the artistic patrimony of the Dutch. These kinds of examples, however, apply only when there are well-defined property rights to specific assets. The motivations behind these behaviors won't spur us to preserve the environment or maximize the rate of sustainable economic growth. Once again, the proper depth of concern for the more distant future does not come to us automatically, at least not in a wide variety of cases.

Expressed differently, when it comes to non-tradable and storable assets, markets do not reflect the preferences of currently unborn individuals. The branch of economics known as welfare economics holds up perfect markets as a normative ideal, yet future generations cannot contract in today's markets. If we were to imagine future generations engaging in such contracting, current decisions might run more in their favor. Circa 2018, the future people of 2068 can't express their preferences across a lot of the choices we are making today, such as how rapidly to boost future wealth or how much to mitigate the risk of serious catastrophes.[4]

Let's now consider some basic choices about how to value the distant future. Again, think of a decision-maker weighing present and future interests, in this case human lives. The way discounting works, if we discount the future by five percent, a person's death today is worth about thirty-nine billion deaths five hundred years from now. Alternatively, at that same discount rate, one death two hundred years from now is equal in value to 131.5 deaths three hundred years from now. Upon reflection, few people, putting aside their selfish interest in the current time period, would share these conclusions as a basis for ethical decision-making.[5]

---

4. To see how this works, consider a much wealthier future one hundred years from now. In spite of higher overall wealth, some individuals might die from current decisions, such as environmental neglect. If those individuals could bid on today's policies, they would bid for greater concern for the future. If we think of the growth of wealth as (roughly) matching the interest or discount rate, their bids, in today's terms, would carry about as much weight as ours. And if the policy had the potential to make a big impact on their lives, future generations could well be the dominant bidders in a policy evaluation. Yet current market prices are not giving them any weight, or are giving them weight only through our imperfect altruism. Think of this as further evidence that current methods are undervaluing the allocation of resources to future generations.

5. On how individuals respond to queries about current and future lives, see Frederick (2003, 2006).

Or consider the comparison prospectively. Under any positive discount rate, no matter how low, one life today could be worth more than one million lives in the future. It could even be worth the entire subsequent survival of the human race, if we use a long enough time horizon for the comparison. At the very least, we should be skeptical that positive discount rates apply to every choice before us. Sometimes we should be less impatient and pay the future greater heed.

Even if you think that individual impatience is sometimes justified, impatience will not justify the positive discounting of well-being across generations. Time preference may mean that an individual prefers to have a good steak dinner sooner rather than later. Even if this is rational—after all, you're getting hungrier by the minute—this kind of time preference doesn't apply across longer time frames, including future generations. Our still-unborn great-great-grandchildren will not receive benefits for some time. But in the meantime they are not sitting around, waiting impatiently with rumbling stomachs. It cannot be argued that their forthcoming slice of time is worth less simply because they must wait for it. Similarly, it cannot be argued that Medieval peasants benefited from having been born before us and thus having eaten their bread sooner. When we consider long periods of time and count the years before individuals are born, we need to discard impatience as a factor of relevance because it just doesn't apply. Time preference therefore does not justify the significant discounting of the distant future, even if it justifies Tom's wanting to have his steak dinner sooner rather than later.[6]

Another way of thinking about why a high time discount rate is wrong involves a somewhat unusual—some would say kooky—thought experiment. Einstein's theory of relativity suggests that

6. Note, by the way, that individual time preference is a tricky concept. What if I am very hungry and wish to eat now rather than later? Does this count as time preference? Or does time preference imply that the same "eating experience"—holding the level of hunger constant—should be preferred sooner rather than later? If we hold everything constant, in what sense can we even say that time has passed? So the passage of time means that ceteris paribus clauses cannot be totally strict, but then we return to the question of what should vary with the postulated passage of time. Arguably all instances of "goods in different time periods" are simply different goods, noting that economists define "goods" in terms of revealed preference and indifference. These messy problems haven't been cleaned up, but they do cast further doubt on the idea of the rationality of purely positive time preference per se.

there is no one factual answer to the question, "What time is it?" Any measurement of time (when is "now"?) is relative to the perspective of an observer, and to the velocity of that observer relative to the speed of light. In other words, if you are traveling very fast, you are moving into the future at an especially rapid rate. Yet it seems odd, to say the least, to discount the well-being of people as their velocity increases. If, for instance, we sent off a spacecraft at nearly the velocity of light, the astronauts would return to Earth, hardly aged, many millions of years hence. Should we pay less attention to the safety of our spacecraft, and thus to the welfare of our astronauts, the faster those vehicles go? Should we—as a result of positive discounting—not give them enough fuel to make a safe landing? And if you decline to condemn these brave astronauts to death, how are they different from other residents of the distant future?

Instead of letting our speedy astronauts die, we can think of the universe as a block of four-dimensional space-time. We would not discount human well-being for temporal distance per se any more than we would discount well-being for spatial location per se. In moral terms, maybe time really is an illusion, as Buddha suggested thousands of years ago.

That said, discounting for risk is justified in a way that discounting for the pure passage of time is not. If a future benefit is uncertain, we should discount that benefit accordingly because it may not arrive. But such a practice does not dent a deep concern for the distant future. It is precisely because we discount for risk that we seek to protect our future against great tragedies, thereby making that future less risky. If we boost the long-term sustainable growth rate, for instance, we are indeed making the future less risky. Rather than ignoring risk, a future-oriented perspective takes long-term risk into account and attempts to lower it. The factor of risk might encourage you to spend your money now, otherwise someone might steal it. But it won't discourage us from caring a lot about long-term sustainable growth.

Before moving on, let's consider the relevance of the numerical comparisons presented above of events which lie one hundred, two hundred, or even five hundred years into the future. It might seem that nothing we do today can affect the world that far out, most of all when it comes to policy issues. Yet the most recent evidence suggests that good (or bad) political and economic decisions, and the general existence of prosperity, have persistent effects that stretch for centuries into the future. Colonial policies from the sixteenth and seventeenth centuries have persistent effects on prosperity today, and there is even research suggesting that the prosperity of a region well before the birth of Christ holds predictive power for the prosperity of those regions today.[7]

For whatever reason, good institutions and a history of prosperity tend to have enduring effects. Wealth can fund and enable better government, and that in turn gives rise to further wealth and better institutions. Institutional memories of economic success and good governance can persist for long periods of time. Cultural practices such as business savvy or an interest in external markets can last for centuries.

England, which led the Industrial Revolution, had positive institutional features stretching far back in its history, such as relatively free labor markets in Medieval times and the carving out of a coherent national unit with a language, an army, and a parliament. The practices of the empire then carried some of these institutions across the oceans, such as when the British settled much of North America and the Antipodes (though not every region benefited from the brighter side of British rule). It's no accident that many of the original territories of the Roman Empire remain some of the world's wealthiest and most successful nations. China was also a relatively wealthy nation in

---

7. Spolaore and Wacziarg (2013) survey this research. Acemoglu, Johnson, and Robinson (2001, 2002, 2005) show how decisions and institutions from the early colonial era still affect economic performance today. Comin, Easterly, and Gong (2010) show the extent to which regional wealth in 1000 B.C. still predicts regional wealth today.

earlier times, and that prosperity is reemerging today. For centuries, Chinese entrepreneurs around the world have shown special commercial savvy; this again has something to do with history.

Of course, the persistence of prosperity does not apply in every case. Much of the Arab world is currently well below its historic relative standing; Baghdad might have been one of the best and most interesting cities to live in about a thousand years ago, but today it is struggling. Still, if we think in terms of averages, we see plenty of evidence that history can matter over very long time spans. Therefore, any act which strengthens good institutions today has, in expected value terms, a causal stretch running centuries into the future. Once again, this means that our choice of discount rate is of critical importance.

We can also see the importance of faith to the overall argument. To fully grasp the import of doing the right thing, and the importance of creating wealth and strengthening institutions, we must look very deeply into the distant future. As I have argued at length, this is a conclusion suggested by reason. But in the real world of actual human motivations, the application of abstract reason across such long time horizons is both rare and unhelpful when it comes to getting people to do the right thing. The actual attitudes required to induce an acceptance of such long time horizons are, in psychological terms, much closer to a kind of faith. We cannot see these very distant expected gains, but we must believe in them nonetheless, and we must hold those beliefs near and dear to our hearts. In this sense, we should strongly reject the modern secular tendency to claim that a good politics can or should be devoid of faith.

There are, of course, many bad forms of faith in politics, and we should not encourage political (or other) beliefs in willful disregard of reason. But we cannot kick away faith itself as a motivational tool, as politics is of necessity built on some kind of faith. The lack—and, indeed, the sometimes conscious rejection—of the notion of faith, as is common in secular rationalism, is one of the most troubling features of the contemporary world. It has brought us some very real gains in terms of personal freedom, but it also threatens to diminish our ability to make the very best choices.

Should we discount the *past?*

So far we've been considering how much the future is worth compared to the present. But there's another way to approach the problem of time, and that is to ask how much the past is worth compared to the present. That's the dilemma we face when questions arise about restitution for past injustices, such as past theft or slavery. In these cases, we must ask ourselves how much a past cost should count for in the present.

One approach to restitution problems applies a standard rate of positive discount to the previous costs to convert them into a present value. Let's say the discount rate is seven percent. If my ancestor stole a thousand dollars from your ancestor back in the year 1854, I should have to pay you seven percent compounded for each year between 1854 and 2018. Presumably that would undo this harm or rectify the injustice. But if you do the math, that amounts to more than $65 million. Most observers would correctly judge that such a restitutional award would be excessive. If the theft had not occurred, it is unlikely that you or your descendants would have had anything approaching that sum today. In fact, given how easily inheritances are squandered, you'd be lucky to have anything at all. Furthermore, no matter how loudly you proclaim the justice of this transfer, I don't have the millions to give you. If we are going to award restitution at all, the amount of the initial theft plus some modest premium for suffering is more realistic.[8]

The upshot is this: when we work from the past toward the present, we generally don't—and shouldn't—apply a standard rate of positive discount to make the later period of time less valuable. Again, a posi-

8. Cowen (1997) pursues these questions.

tive rate of discount cannot be applied uncritically, especially over long periods of time.

Yet another argument pushes us toward relatively low discount rates. Not all values are economic values, and the pluralist bundle will likely contain what are called ideal goods, merit goods, and possibly Platonic values. By definition, these goods are not derived from individual preferences; rather, they refer to something which is objectively good for its own sake, according to some moral theory. For instance, when it comes to the value of Platonic beauty, we care that it exists at all; we care less about exactly which consumers have access to it when. Non-preference values seem to be the least eligible candidates for strong temporal discounting, and so a concern for non-preference values will strengthen the weight we should place on the future relative to the present.

Maybe you're not persuaded by these arguments. It's difficult to ask serious economic and philosophic questions about the world five hundred years from now, or even a hundred years from now. The Einstein's theory example was weirder still. Even talking about time preference across generations is confusing. So we don't have a clear argument that the discount rate for human well-being should be exactly zero. But still, some significant holes have been punched in the idea that we should discount the distant future at very high rates and thereby assign it much less importance in our calculations.

The opportunity cost argument

Some economists offer the opportunity cost argument for discounting resource flows or dollars, and forgive me for a page or two because this becomes slightly technical.[9] This argument notes that investing a dollar today at positive returns will yield more than a dollar next year. Capital is generally productive. So a dollar today is worth more than a dollar in the future because the dollar today can be invested for more than a dollar tomorrow. In economic terms, the

---

9. See Lind et al. (1982), Arrow et al. (1994), Broome (1994), Brennan (2007), and Gollier (2013). Cowen (2007) also discusses these issues.

positive interest rate equalizes marginal rates of substitution over time, or, in other words, it expresses the value of a future dollar relative to a current dollar. This argument does not require positive time preference.

This argument, by the way, does not suggest that we accept observed market interest rates uncritically as a measure of how much we should discount the future. We must adjust market interest rates for risk, transaction costs, and other complicating factors, such as taxes. Still, the market rate of interest would be a rough starting point for thinking about how much to discount the future.[10]

The opportunity cost argument expresses a powerful logic, but, if understood properly, it does not militate against caring deeply about the distant future.

First, the economic arguments deal with wealth only; these arguments do not establish strong positive discounting across *well-being*. If a higher rate of sustainable growth boosts well-being over time, it's the well-being we care about. And we shouldn't discount future well-being, even if we see reasons for discounting material resources or future income streams. Well-being is an end in itself, but wealth is a conduit to well-being and other plural values. For the most important part of the pluralist bundle—well-being—our deep concern for the distant future continues to hold. If we can produce ongoing gains in human well-being for the future, we have our Crusonia plant, and the case for maximizing sustainable growth remains.

Second, even putting well-being aside, the whole point of the opportunity cost argument is that material wealth today can be invested and earn a positive rate of return, at least on average. That's a good

---

10. This argument for discounting is more complex than is sometimes recognized. It does not require time preference, but it does require assumptions about the intertemporal substitutability of consumption. Diminishing marginal utility, in the classic sense, is defined at a single point in time. But how do differing marginal utilities of consumption vary across time? How does my two millionth dollar next year compare to my one millionth dollar today? This variable is distinct from either classic time preference or classic diminishing marginal utility. For the classic economic argument to work, it is usually assumed that consumption tomorrow is a relatively close substitute for consumption today.

argument for substantial investment in the future; it is not an argument for caring *less* about the future.

Another argument for strong discounting of the future is that those individuals will be better off or wealthier than we are today. But even if we take the egalitarian premise of this argument for granted, it will lead to discounting for wealth rather than across time. The discounting would apply to today's wealthy people, too, but our deep concern for the distant future will continue to hold. For one thing, a lot of individuals, even in the future, probably won't be wealthy at all, or at least they won't be wealthy unless we do the right thing. In essence we are choosing their wealth through current policies (if we choose properly), so we should not assume their wealth as a justification for neglecting them. Or maybe they're wealthy for most of their lives, but they're not very wealthy when faced with extreme tragedy or serious illness. No matter how bright the future may seem, it's still going to yield an ongoing stream of human tragedies. The way to minimize those tragedies, again, is to maximize sustainable growth.

Rather than opting for a strictly zero discount rate, I suggest a more modest postulate, one to which I already have referred but will now label formally: **Deep Concern for the Distant Future**. In this view, we should not count catastrophic losses for much less simply because those losses are temporally distant. In the absence of qualifying factors, no amount of temporal distance per se should cause major widespread tragedies to dwindle into insignificance in the present. We should believe that the end of the world is a truly terrible event, even if that collapse comes in the distant future. Similarly, the continued persistence of civilization three hundred years from now is *much* better than having no further civilization at that point in time. A much wealthier future civilization is much better than a less wealthy future civilization. Those are the implications of a deep concern for the distant future.

If you are technically and mathematically minded, you can later read Appendix A, in which I lay out a version of what is called the overtaking criterion. That is one formal way to pin down a deep concern for the distant future, but you don't need mathematics to grasp the intuition. The overtaking criterion implies the following: given the long-run comovement of sustainable growth and human well-being, if one growth path is consistently higher than the other over time, we should prefer that higher growth path. At some point in the future, the higher growth rate will make people much, much better off, and that path is worth choosing even if it involves some cost in terms of foregone consumption today.

The overtaking criterion pushes us toward maximizing Wealth Plus, as defined in the previous chapter, yet without committing to the idea that future well-being is worth *exactly* as much as current well-being. So the overtaking criterion is not a final or definitive moral view on how to compare present and future values in each and every circumstance. Rather it represents one practical rule, a kind of minimum commitment to the future of human well-being. I'll discuss this more in Appendix A, but for now I recommend simply pocketing the intuition and moving on to the next chapter.

Why eat an ice cream cone when someone in Malawi is starving? That's one version of an age-old question in ethics, yet it remains difficult to answer.

Under any moral theory which counts the interests of people in a more or less cosmopolitan manner, our personal obligations toward the poor appear strong. For instance, several billion people in the world currently live on less than two dollars a day. Last year millions of children died of preventable diseases such as diarrhea or experienced stunted growth and development. Presented with these examples, it's easy to feel like we should all be attending to such problems with more resources and more energy than we do now, and indeed we should. The more difficult question, however, is how far such obligations extend and whether such obligations should prevent us from pursuing our own more personal or more individualistic goals. In contrast to utilitarianism, common sense morality typically suggests that we do have the right to pursue our own lives and life plans.

By some accounts of our obligations to others, every individual is obliged to work a certain number of years for charity, or to send most of his or her income to the poor. Wealthy doctors should spend large parts of their careers, if not their entire careers, in African villages. Many more of us would have to become doctors or nurses, unless of course you would be more effective as a Wall Street wizard and then a wealthy philanthropist. Maybe these options sound meritorious to you, but how far are you willing to go to act on your beliefs? Are you willing to value the interests of others on par with your own, or those of your family and friends? If you buy into the standard utilitarian logic of beneficence, a mother might have to abandon or sell her baby in order to raise money to send food to the babies of others. At this point most people balk at the argument and search for some moral principle that limits our obligations to the very poor.

One problem is that the needs of the suffering are so enormous that only a few able or wealthy individuals would be able to carry out individual life projects of their own choosing. Most people would instead become a kind of utility slave, serving only the interests of others and feeding themselves just enough to survive. The result is that utilitarianism—or many forms of consequentialism, for that matter—is often seen as an excessively demanding moral philosophy. People fall into two camps: those who reject utilitarianism for its extreme and unacceptable implications, and those, like the early Peter Singer, who trumpet the call for greater sacrifice and pursue the utilitarian logic to a consistent extreme.

As I stated earlier, I am a pluralist rather than a simple utilitarian. Still, utility is a central and important value, so I would like to confront these dilemmas and consider the scope of our obligations to the poor. I don't, however, wish to focus on government vs. private charity. To be sure, that is an important practical issue, but I'll instead focus on the broader conceptual question of whether growth or redistribution—in the public or private sector—is a more effective means of helping the poor. When framed in this manner, we'll see that there are some strong and strict limits on our obligations to redistribute wealth, even if we accept a full utilitarian framework. In other words, I'll end up siding with common sense morality, which (mostly) allows us to pursue individual life goals.

It can be argued very plausibly and, I think, correctly that we are obliged to help the poor more than we are doing now. But the correct approach to our cosmopolitan obligations does not lead to personal enslavement or massive redistribution of our personal wealth. Most of us should work hard, be creative, be loyal to our civilization, build healthy institutions, save for the future, contribute to an atmosphere of social trust, be critical when necessary, and love our families. Our strongest obligations are to contribute to sustainable economic growth and to support the general spread of civilization, rather than to engage in massive charitable redistribution in the narrower sense. In the longer run, greater economic growth and a more stable civilization will help the poor most of all.

This point can be expressed as follows: we should redistribute wealth only up to the point that it maximizes the rate of sustainable economic growth. This may mean more redistribution than we currently undertake, and sometimes redistribution of a different kind, namely growth-enhancing redistribution. (By no means do all of today's government programs actually redistribute wealth to the poor, much less boost economic growth.) It will not, however, suggest that a utilitarian or consequentialist approach obliges us to redistribute most of our nation's income to the very poor. Nor are productive individuals morally required to spend most of their years serving the very poor.

There nonetheless remains a good case to be made for some degree of redistribution. For instance, a well-constructed welfare state can distribute education and nutrition more widely. The individuals supported by this state are not only better off, but they are more likely to be productive and pay taxes, and they are less likely to overturn public order. Other benefits of redistribution stem from political improvements. Social welfare programs can buy the loyalties of special interest groups and decrease feelings of desperation, both of which can help cement social order. Furthermore, social welfare programs make many citizens feel better about their state, again boosting public order as well as political consensus and stability.[1]

These factors rationalize some investments in a welfare state—and yes, we should describe them as investments—and thus support some

---

1. See for instance Alesina and Rodrik (1994) and Persson and Tabellini (1994). For a survey of the growing literature on how income distribution can affect growth, see Greiner, Semmler, and Gong (2005, 132-133).

wealth redistribution. Furthermore, they suggest an appropriate nature and scope for such redistribution, namely that we try to enhance sustainable economic growth.

Past some margin, an overly generous level of wealth transfer harms economic growth. Many people end up working less, or working less hard, and the associated higher tax rates discourage entrepreneurship and can lead to economic stasis. Furthermore, if it is standard procedure to approach government for a handout, that will induce too much rent-seeking, dependency, corruption, and eventually fiscal imbalances and perhaps even insolvency or a financial crisis. Alternatively, excess or poorly conceived welfare expenditures may create urban cultures of dependency and crime, which endanger social order. The empirical literature suggests that non-infrastructure government spending is correlated positively with lower growth rates, with the caveat that those results are measuring traditional GDP rather than an alternative notion such as Wealth Plus.[2]

Excess transfers are bad for another reason, namely that they make it harder to absorb high numbers of immigrants from poorer countries. Whether rationally or not, many voters feel that migrants are a burden on the government budget, and they resent it when some immigrants receive government benefits. To be sure, some level of social welfare makes immigration run more smoothly by helping immigrants to become established and self-sufficient. But too high a level of benefits is likely to mean, one way or another, a lower level of migration and a corresponding reduction in the most effective anti-poverty program we have discovered to date. This too should limit our attachment to social welfare programs.[3]

---

2. See, for instance, Barro (1991). Goodin, Headey, Muffels, and Dirven (1999) argue that a democratic social welfare state does not lower the rate of economic growth, but they use only two data points, the Netherlands and the United States. See also Lindert (2004). He argues that higher welfare spending tends to be packaged with other growth–enhancing policies, such as low taxation on capital income. He does not show that higher spending at Western European levels is itself good for economic growth.

3. On utilitarian obligations, see Scarre (1996). In addition to Smart and Williams (1973), Rand (1967), Scheffler (1982), Wolf (1982), Railton (1984), and Nagel (1986) also criticize the notion of extreme utilitarian obligations.

So rather than redistributing most wealth, we can do better for the world by investing in high-return activities like supporting immigration and producing new technologies with global reach, such as cell phones and new methods for boosting agricultural productivity. Many people mock the term "trickle-down economics," but most social benefits do take a trickle-down form. We should of course prefer a flood to a trickle, which brings us back to wishing to boost the sustainable growth rate as much as possible.

These stipulated individual obligations are not so far from common sense morality. To be sure, we have not yet bridged the gap between utilitarian reasoning and common sense morality. Even when utilitarianism and common sense recommend the same course of action, they do so for different reasons. Utilitarianism tells us we should work, save, and innovate to serve the purposes of others, including future generations. Common sense morality tells us we should work and save to take care of our families and because we value our own lives. These two perspectives remain distinct in their methods and their justifications. Nonetheless, to the extent that the practical conclusions converge, we can think of utilitarian and common sense modes of reasoning as two aspects of some broader moral picture. After all, I favor pluralism rather than utilitarianism or common sense morality per se. So we do not have to bring these two perspectives into complete accord. Instead, for the purpose of constructing a workable pluralism, it may suffice to know that two of the tools in our toolbox point in broadly compatible directions.[4]

We can now consider the question of why public and private ethical codes might differ so much in their recommendations. In the private sphere, virtually everyone would agree that a mother is justified in looking after her own baby rather than selling it to send resources to the babies of strangers. Yet in the public sphere, it is widely believed that governments should be more impartial, at least within national boundaries.[5] Governments should not favor the interests of one par-

4. Hurley (2009) raises the question of whether consequentialism, even if it stipulates that some set of actions is good, can generate a strong obligation to perform those actions. In the synthetic view outlined here, that sense of obligation can come from common sense morality, if need be.

5. See Goodin (1995).

ticular baby over another, at least not for the same reasons that a mother would favor her baby over a stranger's.

But why should morality be so bifurcated? Simply reiterating the existence of our intuitions won't justify that practice. But within the framework of this book, perhaps we can see why moral obligations vary between an individual acting in a private capacity and a government acting in the interest of increasing the rate of sustainable economic growth. This is actually just another application of Adam Smith's classic principle of the division of labor. It's easy to see why parents do best when they attend to their family priorities and governments do best when they institute a legal regime based on impartiality and the rule of law. Again, I'm not suggesting that this argument provides an exact justification for the intricacies of common sense morality as it is appears in the world, with all of its quirks and custom-dependent variations. I'm simply noting that the gap between common sense morality and utility maximization, properly construed, is much smaller than it might at first appear.

We can test these hypotheses by looking for cases in which a utilitarian or a consequentialist *should* favor large-scale redistribution toward the very poor. For instance, the case for redistribution would be stronger if the world were going to end in the near future. If the time horizon is extremely short, the benefits of continued higher growth will be choked off and the scope for compounding over time would be correspondingly limited. The immediate returns to charity should therefore weigh more heavily in the decision calculus. To present this point in its starkest form, imagine that the world were set to end tomorrow. There would be little point in maximizing the growth rate; arguably, we should just throw a party and consume what we can (after feeding the hungry, that is).

Alternatively, the real return on investment might be permanently negative or zero. In this case, compounding of returns would not operate, a long time horizon would not lead to a Crusonia plant, and there would again be greater incentive to redistribute wealth. A high degree of redistribution also makes sense in a lot of "lifeboat" settings, where, for example, a group of desperate individuals are afloat on the open sea and are wondering how to share the cans of Spam. These examples typically involve an implicit assumption of a zero or negative rate of return on investment, or perhaps investment simply isn't possible in such an artificial setting. Again, there isn't a Crusonia plant to chase after.

The attitude of *historical pessimism* is therefore one of the most important critiques of my arguments. If historical pessimism holds true, as is suggested by many old-school conservatives, expected rates of return are negative, there are no long-lasting Crusonia plants, and my arguments, even if they hold up logically, do not apply. Historical pessimism is therefore much more than a mood or an attitude; if true, it would shape our substantive views and our practical choices significantly. But for the purposes of Crusonia plant arguments, positive economic growth need only be possible *with some probability*; this is an argument whose underlying structure recurs throughout these chapters. That positive probability means that the growth calculus will dominate our estimates of the expected returns from different choices. We can therefore reject the final practical stance of the historical pessimists, even as we recognize that they often get the better of the optimists in the substantive arguments about the future course of our world.

The current political opinions of social scientists do not always match up with these conclusions. Many advocates of greater state spending—especially non-economists—seem to like the idea of a very low discount rate. Many of these individuals would like our government to devote more resources to education, to infrastructure, and to improving the environment, all positions associated with the political left overall, at least in the United States. They see a lower discount rate as supporting all of these policies. Yet they also tend to favor redistribution, even when such policies conflict with economic growth. In this sense the political left does not have a consistent attitude toward the importance of the future. Many thinkers on the right suffer from the opposite inconsistency. They often favor market-based discount rates, which are relatively high, but when the topic is redistribution, they worry much more about the longer-term consequences.[6]

In contrast, I see a deep concern for the distant future as cutting across the political spectrum. A greater orientation toward the future is likely to increase the desirability of policies favoring a market economy, economic growth, and technological innovation. Furthermore, some of the arguments for these institutions may in fact require a deep concern for the more distant future. For instance, positive rates of discount usually imply that we should grant considerable importance to the alleviation of immediate suffering. Market liberalizations, whatever long-run virtues they may have, sometimes increase immediate suffering because they require resource reallocations, namely that many workers must try to find new jobs. Furthermore, market economies often invest their surpluses in long-run growth, rather than redistributing funds to the immediately suffering poor.

Market economies and market reforms look better as more weight is placed on the relatively distant future. A free society is better today than a corrupt and totalitarian one. But one hundred years from now, the difference in human welfare and other relevant values will prove far more pronounced. Over time the United States gained ground on the Soviet Union, rather than allowing convergence.

Who should sacrifice, and when?
Under more normal circumstances, with a long time horizon, a utilitarian or consequentialist framework may still recommend that some individuals sacrifice significant parts of their lives, or risk such sacri-

---

6. For a left–wing view of discounting, see, for instance, Solow (1974). Beckerman (1996) offers a market–oriented view critical of zero discounting.

fices, for the greater social good. To cite a simple example, Martin Luther King Jr. brought much good to the world with respect to both justice and long-term economic growth. It would be fair to say that King did the right thing in choosing to pursue higher ideals rather than playing golf all day, even though he lost his life in doing so. The same can be said of Gandhi. Nonetheless, such obligations to sacrifice cannot be universal or near-universal. If we all went around sacrificing our own individualistic pursuits to an extreme degree, there would be no civilization left to advance. As we saw earlier, it is more sensible to reject collective sacrificial recommendations that will lower the rate of sustainable economic growth.

In many cases our obligations should be viewed at a collective level. This framework does not pin down a uniquely correct course of action for each individual, so it's not morally clear which individual is obliged to make the sacrifice. What if there were an innocent girl drowning in a lake, and any one of us could jump in and save her? In these cases the question, "What should I do?" allows for considerable latitude, and the scope of my individual obligation, as a group member, may be indeterminate. It's good if I risk my safety and jump in after her, but it's also fine if someone else does it instead. Similarly, it doesn't have to be *my* group that protests government injustice, because many other groups could do this as well. This becomes a problem of game theory, and as we know from game theory, the implied obligation of a single individual or group is very often indeterminate.

Imagine a game with payoffs, so that it is better if someone makes a sacrifice to achieve a socially valuable end, but it is worse if everyone sacrifices or tries to sacrifice to achieve that end. The structure of this problem is common to many questions of morality and individual obligation, including the problem of global poverty. Some people should make sacrifices to help out, but, because we must keep our economically advanced civilization up and running, not everyone should make such sacrifices. Arguably this is the paradigmatic payoff structure with which to address questions related to global poverty, sacrifice, and obligation.

A utilitarian standard, in its simplest form, would suggest that the "least cost supplier" should make such a sacrifice. That moves us a little bit closer to common sense morality, namely by stipulating that the sacrificers should be the people most inclined to do so. This would include saints, moral saints, and dedicated agents of social change, as well as individuals who, for whatever reason, don't find the required sacrifices to be so very daunting.

If several potential sacrificers face the same cost and can produce the same expected social benefits from their sacrifice, then it can be said that one of them (or, more broadly, some subset of them) *should* sacrifice. In these cases it is morally indeterminate who should sacrifice and who should not, or who should move to Malawi to administer vaccinations to children. This is less oppressive, and less antagonistic to individual life plans, than the typical utilitarian scenarios involving enslaved Western doctors toiling away to suit purposes other than their own.

When confronted with global poverty or other forms of calamity, many (or most) people express something along the lines of, "Well, *someone* ought to do something." At the same time, they do not feel strongly that this "someone" ought to be themselves. Such intuitions may seem incoherent or perhaps even selfishly irresponsible. But they match up to one of the realities of this game. Yes, *someone* ought to do *something*, but the game itself does not make clear who that someone is. The result is an under-provision of the public good and that many people continue to make the assumption, largely for selfish reasons, that this "someone" is going to be someone else. My point is not that the observed response is socially optimal, only that the best solution to the game corresponds to some underlying features of common sense morality.[7]

7. Alternatively, a sacrificer could be specified by lot. Or we could look to game theory. We could think of morality as prescribing that individuals should play what economists call randomized Nash strategies, which will mean some probability of selfishness and some probability of sacrifice for each individual, as if we were rolling a die. A correctly specified randomization strategy will

In any case, individuals are more likely to sacrifice too little than too much, and too few individuals are willing to sacrifice much at all. So we can look to a specific recommendation of another kind, even if it cannot always help us calculate which individual should perform a given sacrifice. We should strengthen our consciences, as well as social norms, to increase the probability that the appropriate individuals would be willing to make a needed sacrifice if it turned out to be best, all things considered, that they be the one to step forward. We ought to honor and reward such sacrifices more in order to increase their likelihood. Again, this is not so far from common sense morality.

Should money be redistributed to the rich?

In many cases, purely utilitarian prescriptions will have morally counterintuitive implications, but ones that run counter to the usual concerns about enslaved American doctors serving poor Africans. Namely, utilitarianism may support the transfer of resources from the poor to the rich. A talented entrepreneur, for instance, can probably earn a higher rate of return on invested resources than can a disabled great-grandmother. Indeed, a common complaint in the literature on inequality is that the rich get richer while the poor get poorer, or at least more or less stay put. If this portrait is to be believed, then the rich earn higher returns on their accumulated wealth, as has been argued by the French economist Thomas Piketty. If we combine the trickle-down effect from the wealth of the wealthy with a zero rate of discount, it is easy to generate scenarios in which utilitarianism would recommend the redistribution of wealth to the wealthy.

For instance, let's assume, for the sake of argument, that the wealthy earn eight percent on their holdings, annually and on average, while the poor earn one percent. If one-fifth of the gains to the wealthy trickle down to the poor over time, then the poor are better off if the wealthy command more resources. They will receive one-fifth of the eight percent, or 1.6 percent, rather than the one percent they would earn on their own. Usually this trickle won't reach them right away,

bring about the right amount of sacrifice—on average, at least—without requiring everybody to sacrifice. The proper randomized set of strategies will be those that maximize sustainable, expected global economic growth.

but over time the rich will build more factories, buy more products, hire more domestic workers, fund more research and development, push for more immigration, and so on. Sooner or later, many among the poor will benefit. If we have a deep concern for the distant future, it matters less if most of these benefits come later.

The implications of this redistribution to the rich will be anti-egalitarian at first, but over a sufficiently long time horizon the poor will benefit increasingly from the high rate of economic growth. The results need not be anti-egalitarian if we consider the appropriate stretch of time, but they are sure to appear anti-egalitarian by many common metrics, which focus only on the short run or on a single country rather than adopting an appropriately longer, broader, and more global perspective.

I am not suggesting that a good pluralist theory will endorse major systematic redistribution of wealth to the wealthy or the talented. For one thing, this may be one case in which a rights constraint limits the core recommendation of growth maximization. Maybe it's just not *right* for a hedge fund manager to seize resources from a bricklayer, no matter how good an investor the manager may be. An alternative concern, one that would also limit redistribution to the wealthy, is that a sufficiently unequal distribution of wealth may lead to lower growth through a number of the channels discussed above.

What's important, however, is how this reframing shifts the burden of proof by examining the implications of a very low discount rate. Direct, short-term redistribution to today's poor is no longer the default option for a moral theory that emphasizes individual well-being. Instead, in many cases utilitarianism has to work to avoid the conclusion of redistributing more resources to the wealthy. Once again, it is possible to have a moral theory which focuses on good consequences without requiring everyone to give up eighty percent of their income or to work as a doctor in Africa.[8]

8. On our obligations to save, see Rawls (1999, 252).

Finally, we need to think carefully about where the most significant gains of the past have come from, and we should emphasize the extension of those gains rather than redistribution per se. Arguably the most important gifts of the past generation to the current generation come from wise investments, a belief in rules of just conduct, good political institutions, and good values, among other related historical factors. Growth-enhancing institutions do require hard work, but that investment is a positive-sum rather than a zero-sum game across the generations. The resulting moral impulse is one of strengthening good rules conducive to future economic growth, properly understood, and here again we approach a common sense morality.

Our obligations to the elderly
Given the limits on our obligations to the poor, we will have comparable limits on our obligations to the elderly. In fact, we can think of the elderly as individuals who are poor in one particular dimension, namely in their future human capital. The elderly are more likely to die soon than are the young. And while we should do a good deal to help the elderly, the logic of sustainable growth places limits on these obligations, too.

There is a more general question here about how much a consequentialist or utilitarian standard should value the lives of the elderly. I recall a job interview in 1986 in which I was asked by my interviewer, the economist Julius Margolis, "Why don't we value human lives at replacement cost?" I was caught off guard and didn't have a good answer for him. Yet his challenge sounded so wrong to me. Don't the elderly deserve more respect than that? Do they not experience special lives, the value of which cannot be captured by metaphors of replacement? I've been thinking about that question for a long time because it challenges a lot of our moral intuitions.

Let's start with a simple example. If a house is worth $1 million in the marketplace but it can be built anew at a replacement cost of

$500,000, then the correct value of the house is $500,000, at least provided we actually take action to replace it. To make that more concrete, we should not spend $800,000 to save the house from destruction when we can replace it with a perfect replica at a cost of $500,000.

So let's say a human life is worth $4 million, as estimated by standard economic willingness to pay to reduce risk measures, but we can create another human life for about $10,000, say by subsidizing births or by saving another human life in a more economical manner elsewhere. Birth subsidies are probably going to be cheaper than spending $4 million to save a life. So how much should we spend to save or preserve that first human life? Should we spend $4 million? Or is this human life worth only $10,000—in other words, its replacement cost?

Virtually all of us would agree that $10,000—it could be even less—is not, in general, an adequate valuation of a life, including the life of an elderly person. For one thing, the life we would lose and the new life we would create would not be identical. So we would not, strictly speaking, be replacing the life that has been lost. We may also feel a special obligation toward older individuals by virtue of their roles in raising us, building our nation, and defending us in earlier wars. Furthermore, failing to save the first life and investing in helping or creating another life are not usually causally related. Letting an elderly person die rather than spending money to save their life does not automatically activate higher birth subsidies or other life-saving measures elsewhere in the economy.

So no, it is unlikely that measures of replacement cost are the correct way to value a human life. Still, replaceability should not be completely irrelevant to how we think about the value of a life. If one life disappears and another is added, the new life does make up for *some* of the value lost, at least in utility terms. Argued another way, losing an irreplaceable civilization is a much greater tragedy than losing a civilization in a way which allows for the birth of a new and different one in its place. Replaceability therefore seems to count for something, even if we do not agree for how much.

More practically, the additional wealth that accumulates as a result of economizing on life-saving expenditures does lead people to buy safer cars, to take less risky jobs, and so on. So it can be argued that we will save some number of other lives by investing less in direct life preservation for the elderly. We don't know whether an increment of wealth saved will in fact rescue or preserve other human lives, but *there is some chance that this might be the case*. And this possibility lowers the value of spending a lot of money to extend a human life. So, in a contemporary setting, a human life should probably be valued at less than $4 million, or whatever other sum the willingness to pay method, or some other utilitarian calculation, is going to serve up.

We may not know the exact correct valuation of an individual life, but we do know that the possibility of commensurability, the pull of the more distant future, the ongoing replenishment of human civilization, and the value of investing in future lives, when considered as a whole, exert some downward pressure on how much we should invest in extending the lives of the elderly today. My arguments therefore suggest a lower estimate of the value of a life, including an older life, than most other plausible frameworks, because replacement and replenishment of the civilizational flow are *considered as one factor among many*. Replacement and replenishment should not be taken as the final word, but yes, they do exert downward pressure on our value of life estimates.

To put it more concretely, today in the United States we are spending too much on the elderly and not enough on the young. And given that the elderly are the ones who vote with greatest frequency, and the young often do not or cannot, that mistake should hardly come as a surprise. Governments should focus on investment, but in the United States, at least, government spending on investment is falling; in recent years, government investment has fallen below its postwar average of about five percent. Similar patterns can be observed in many European national budgets.[9] Unfortunately, when government spending needs to be limited or cut, investment is often the first area to go, while entitlements for the elderly remain intact. In this regard, I am suggesting some significant revisions to current trends.

Once-and-for-all changes vs. growth rate changes

Now let's look at one final building block for deciding the appropriate scope of redistribution, namely the nature of economic growth. At a very general level, beneficial policies fall into one of two categories. First, such policies may yield some benefit in a once-and-for-all fashion; imagine increasing the power of all light bulbs for one year. Second, the new benefits may be ongoing and self-augmenting; imagine scientific policies that speed up the rate at which better light bulbs (or other innovations) are developed. Such policies would permanently increase the rate of economic growth; in other words, they would count as a Crusonia plant, a self-generating and self-refreshing source of ongoing value.

When we are examining a policy change or an act of redistribution, it is important to know whether it involves an upfront, once-and-for-all benefit (or cost) or a systematic boost (or decline) in the growth rate over time. This somewhat arcane distinction, drawn from the economic literature on growth, is of great importance for adjudicating potential social changes.

To consider a simple example, many scientists believe that global warming will increase the number of virulent and persistent storms on our planet. Many of these storms may come only after some time, but a greater concern for the future means that we must pay heed to these consequences. More generally, many environmental problems

9. See Harding, McGregor, and Muller (2013).

hurt our prospects for long-run sustained growth. I am suggesting that such problems are especially important.

At the same time, a concern for the distant future can, counterintuitively, dissuade us against certain environmental investments. In contrast to the threat of severe and ongoing storms, some of the costs of climate change take the form of one-time adjustments, such as the cost of relocating coastal settlements. The induced relocation might count as a rights violation of some sort, but from a consequentialist point of view, maximizing the growth rate takes priority over avoiding one-time expenditures and one-time adjustments. Even if those expenditures are large, we will earn back that value over time, due to the logic of compounding growth. So, contrary to what other frameworks might suggest, we should pay greater heed to the storms and less heed to the relocation costs.

It's very important to take note of whether or not a specified policy choice will affect the overall growth rate. The details of this distinction are complicated, however, because economic models provide differing accounts of which changes alter growth rates, as opposed to bringing one-off changes or improvements.

The most prominent economic approach to growth, the Solow model, is named after MIT economist and Nobel Laureate Robert Solow, who laid out the basics of the model in the 1950s. The Solow model postulates a stripped-down economy-wide production function based on constant returns to scale. National output is the result of capital inputs, labor inputs, and technological progress, which renders both capital and labor more effective.[10] In this model, the primary way to increase ongoing growth is to induce a higher rate of technological innovation. Indeed, much empirical research has shown embodied technological progress to be a major factor behind U.S. economic growth.

---

10. See Solow (1956, 1957); Romer (2000) provides a more recent summary.

The Solow model helps us to understand the phenomenon of catch-up growth, which has been so significant in East Asia. In the model, the rate of return on capital diminishes as the capital stock increases. So when there is not much capital, the returns on investment and thus the incentives to invest are high, at least provided that the labor force is of good quality and institutions will protect the property rights of investors. Poorer countries should therefore be expected to catch up to richer countries as they borrow new technologies and increase their capital stocks to implement new and lucrative opportunities. The economic growth in China that began in the 1980s had this catch-up flavor.

The Solow model also implies that economies should recover quickly from one-time negative shocks such as earthquakes or destructive wars. Although the capital stock has fallen from the destruction, the rate of return on capital is now higher precisely because the capital stock has fallen. Additional savings should make up the gap and, over time, restore the economy to its previous growth path. The very rapid recovery of Japan and Germany after World War II demonstrates this mechanism in action. So according to this theory, the rate of growth will remain lower only if the negative shock somehow permanently reduces the rate of technological progress.

For similar reasons, a boost in savings and investment is seen as contributing to transition growth paths but not to steady state growth in the long run. In the model, more savings means a given amount of catch-up growth happens more rapidly, but the savings won't raise long-run growth rates.[11]

That's the Solow model, but I'm not arguing that it is always the best model for understanding our world or for judging redistribution. It is simply one possibility.

---

11. Some later modifications to the Solow model allow for the rates of savings and investment to be correlated with economic growth in a more general manner; see Temple (1999, 139–140). Extensions by Uzawa (1965), Lucas (1988), and others stress the role of human capital in boosting or maintaining the growth rate.

In contrast to the Solow model, the increasing returns model suggests that growth begets more growth. In this view, larger economies should grow more rapidly than smaller economies, and growth rates should continue to increase over time. Improvements beget further improvements and negative events are likewise cumulative, thus the moniker "increasing returns."

Ideas, and their non-rival nature, are often cited as the fundamental source of increasing returns. Once an idea has been generated, it can be used many times by many different people at very low marginal cost. The first idea spreads, begets subsequent ideas, and so growth increases. Or there's another way to look at increasing returns. Larger markets generate stronger incentives for idea production because innovators can sell their product to a larger market (e.g., it would not be worth inventing the iPhone for customers in New Zealand alone). That means large economies can grow more rapidly than small economies. The more the economy grows, the greater the incentive for subsequent new ideas, which in turn reinforces the incentive for growth. New ideas will lead to more growth, which encourages more new ideas, and so on.

The increasing returns model is most commonly associated with the economist Paul Romer, but it can be traced back to Adam Smith and the very beginning of economics as a systematic object of study. In Smith's implicit model, a larger market size supports a greater division of labor, which in turn makes the economy more productive. In other models, greater openness to trade, or a common market area such as the United States, can drive an increasing returns to scale process.

To put these growth theories into my own terminology, the increasing returns model suggests that there are lots and lots of Crusonia plants out there, whereas the Solow model indicates that we can find Crusonia plants only in policies that very directly and very specifically raise the rate of idea generation. The increasing returns model holds that virtually any gain in resources can be translated into higher growth in the long run, rather than washing out in the adjustment process.[12]

Under the increasing returns model, a one-time negative shock harms the long-run rate of growth, which implies that we must take great care to avoid or limit each and every possible negative shock. The Solow model suggests a picture of greater resilience, since catch-up effects prevent each and every mistake from compounding over time into a larger collapse.

The increasing returns growth model will therefore make us more wary of non-growth-enhancing wealth redistribution than will the Solow growth model. In the Solow growth model, the costs of redistribution might be "once-and-for-all," rather than lowering the long-term rate of growth. We can make up for our temporary losses and eventually get back to where we ought to be. In contrast, under the increasing returns model, any setback will make the economy smaller and thus limit future rates of growth, with significant implications for the standard of living in the distant future.

This distinction points to yet another way traditional political debates should be redrawn. Individuals who believe in the increasing returns model should be much more skeptical of non-growth-enhancing redistribution than individuals who believe in the Solow catch-up model.

A central question here is whether the logic of the Solow model or the increasing returns model holds. Even if you don't buy into all of the details of these models, the two core options they present are either that one-time costs do matter a lot in the long run, or they don't. I'm treating the models as stand-ins for these two broader views. The key question is whether gains and losses compound over time or dwindle into longer-run insignificance.[13]

12. On increasing returns models, see Romer (1986, 1990). On the Solow model vs. the increasing returns model, see the 1994 symposium in *Journal of Economic Perspectives*.

13. Neo-institutional approaches are less formal than either the Solow or the increasing returns models. They point to the importance of property rights, well-functioning institutions, trust, the rule of law, and properly aligned microeconomic incentives. Nonetheless, these views do not typi-

Whatever your exact view of the Solow and increasing returns models, the logic of the increasing returns model will likely carry significant weight in our final evaluation. In many cases our best answer, given current knowledge, is that a given cost brings some probability of an ongoing growth effect (as in the increasing returns model) and some probability of a once-and-for-all adjustment cost, followed by catch-up (as in the Solow model). In our expected value calculations, this will operate as an expected impact on the long-term rate of economic growth. Therefore we should incorporate the logic of the increasing returns model into how we evaluate social changes, even if the increasing returns model is not our single best current theory of economic growth. In expected value terms, most of our social choices have an impact upon future rates of economic growth. *Crusonia plants are everywhere*, in expected value terms. We are making decisions about Crusonia plants all the time.

Finally, both the Solow and the increasing returns models emphasize ideas as the wellspring of economic growth. New ideas are the product of human reason; it was Aristotle who defined man as the rational animal. A preoccupation with pursuing growth—or some modified version of the growth ideal—therefore means a preoccupation with ideas, a preoccupation with cultivating human reason, and a preoccupation with the notion that man should realize, perfect, and extend his nature as a generator of powerful ideas that can change the world. Cringe all you wish, but on this point I'll send another credit along to Ayn Rand, who stresses this point even more than most philosophic rationalists. If we are pursuing self-sustaining and self-generating bundles of plural values, we are in one way or another paying homage to the power of human reason.

cally specify which policy changes cause permanent boosts in the growth rate, as opposed to once-and-for-all changes. The neo-institutional models have very real merits in explanatory terms, but for normative purposes they do not mitigate the importance of taking a stance on the long-run growth effects of a policy change. On neo-institutionalist approaches, see Douglass North's work on American and European economic history (North 1981, North and Thomas 1976); see also Olson (1984), Bates et al. (1998), and Acemoglu and Johnson (2004).

When I was a kid, I loved science fiction stories. I loved to think about how things could be totally different from the way they were. One story in particular intrigued me, and I encountered its premise in a few different books. It still appears in popular culture, and if you don't like science fiction, try the 1998 movie *Sliding Doors*, starring Gwyneth Paltrow, which asks how much a single life can be altered by the simple act of missing a train.

The premise is pretty straightforward: if you could somehow manage to go back in time and alter one small event, the entire history of the world might change. One extra sneeze from one caveman millennia ago might overturn life as we know it today. Ray Bradbury's short story "A Sound of Thunder," published in 1952, is one of the early sources of this idea. It seems a little crazy, but the more you think about it, the more it seems to hold true.

The key point is that small changes can very easily turn into big changes. What if Joseph pauses to pick up a penny on the sidewalk? This slight change in the timing of his life will almost certainly alter the particular identities of his future offspring, for example by delaying the occurrence of sexual intercourse with his wife by a tiny increment, or by slightly shifting the position of his testes, thus affecting which sperm will end up fertilizing the eggs of his wife. Further into the future, if a different set of individuals is born, the world will likely take a different path—sometimes a very different path. What if Hitler's great-grandfather had seduced his wife just a moment later in time, changing the combination of sperm and egg that met as a result? Hitler as we know him would never have been born. Even if most people don't much matter for broader aggregate outcomes, it sure seems like some of them do, for instance Jesus or Mohammed or Buddha, not mention Hitler or Lenin. Without Hitler, Nazism probably would not have succeeded; that would mean no World War II and no Holocaust, at least not in the forms we witnessed. Virtually every country's subsequent history would have been different and humanity would be on a very different path for the rest of its time on Earth. Are we really so sure that the United States would still have been the first to build usable nuclear weapons?

You might assume that aggregate global outcomes are mostly stable with respect to small perturbations in the basic events of daily life. You might think, for example, that the logic of positive-sum trade and the power of human reason to advance technological progress will win out in the long run, with or without Hitler on Earth. Other offshoots of these butterfly effects may cancel out or offset each other in the longer run; Tolstoy, in his novel *War and Peace*, argued that the "great men" of history had little impact, as their acts would be reversed by their successors (Napoleon being one case in point).

While part of me wishes that this logic were true, the brute reality is that contingency is real and disturbances to the flow of temporal events need not dwindle into insignificance, given that even a small act can reshape the entire future genetic history of humanity. Napoleon's actions changed the course of life in Germany, which underwent a liberal intellectual revolution as a result of the French invasion and subsequently modernized, as well as Egypt, which received the printing press and a large dose of liberal ideology before starting to resent European interference in local affairs, a feeling that persists to this day. The histories of these regions were changed irrevocably, as were the histories of the Jews who were liberated under Napoleon's rule.

The key point is this: even if you're not convinced that Napoleon really mattered, you don't and indeed can't really know this. There is a real chance that Napoleon being born, rather than a different child from a different act of conception, fundamentally changed world history. So in terms of expected value, it remains the case that small acts can have a big impact on the future, even if they do not always do so. It only has to be the case that some small acts steer the future along a very different path.

Following the philosophers, I refer to this as the epistemic problem.[1] The epistemic problem isn't really about time travel at all, even though science fiction constructs allow us to visualize the problem in an especially vivid manner. The real issue is that we don't know whether our actions today will in fact give rise to a better future, even when it appears that they will. If you ponder these time travel conundrums enough, you'll realize that the effects of our current actions are very hard to predict, and that has nothing to do with whether or not time travel ever becomes possible.

The epistemic critique suggests that the philosophic doctrine of consequentialism cannot be a useful guide to action because we hardly know anything about long-run consequences. While we can try to calculate expected values, such calculations are typically based on a very limited range of information about present consequences or consequences in the near future. As David Schmidtz once put it to me: can

---

1. Lenman (2000) provides one clear statement of the epistemic critique of utilitarianism and cites some precursors. For additional perspectives on the epistemic critique, see also Norcross (1990), Frazier (1994), Howard-Snyder (1997), Dorsey (2012), Mason (2004), Lang (2008), Burch-Brown (2014), and Kolmar and Rommeswinkel (2013). Hayek (1991) can be thought of as offering a version of the epistemic critique as well. Shelly Kagan (1998, 64) calls this epistemic argument "the most common objection to consequentialism." William Whewell provided one early statement of the epistemic critique; see Mill (1969 [1852]). Cowley, Ambrose, and McCullough (2000) consider "what if?" questions in the context of military history. Moriarty (2005) considers the implications of the epistemic argument for concepts of desert. My initial crack at these topics is Cowen (2006). MacAskill (2014) analyzes how we ought to maximize across the expected values of possibly conflicting moral theories with possibly conflicting conceptual frameworks.

we have the correct moral theory if we cannot know ninety percent, or perhaps 99.9 percent, of what counts toward a good outcome?

You would probably agree that it's a good idea to teach teenage drivers not to plough through the yellow light. After all, about forty thousand people die in auto accidents each year in the United States alone. But today, when a driver stops at a yellow light rather than accelerating, he likely affects the length of other people's commutes and thus changes the timing of millions of future conceptions. Subsequent genetic identities will change as well. Come the next generation, these different identities lead to different marriage patterns and thus an entirely new set of individuals in the future. So how can we really tell if our yellow-light rule is a good one? Aren't we operating in the dark? If you think about these conundrums for long enough, you'll start to wonder how we can ever judge good consequences at all.

Once you start worrying about the epistemic problem, you may fear the onset of an extreme moral nervousness. Virtually every action would appear to have enormous consequences for our future. You might fear that maybe, just maybe, you had set in motion the painful deaths of millions the last time you sped through a yellow light; but cheer up, you might have saved millions of others as well. All of those lives rested upon your decision. At any moment, most of us might be doing something that will lead to truly wonderful results, truly terrible results, or, most likely, a mix of both. It seems paralyzing. If you were to internalize that way of thinking, all of life would feel like walking around on eggshells, except that the eggshells are geopolitical changes that might cause millions or even billions of future human lives to be saved or lost.

You may be thinking that this argument is just plain, flat-out stupid. But be patient. I'm not here to defend nihilism or suggest that ethics should focus on the paradoxes of time travel and the timing of conception of the future Hitler. I'd like to defend a version of common sense morality—but first, I do want to look a little more closely at why the epistemic critique does not imply that we should feel hopeless about our efforts to make the world a better place. Once we have that understanding, we'll see that some versions of common sense morality work better than others, and we will move closer to those more sensible forms of common sense morality. That will have some concrete implications. We'll also explore new arguments for some of the positions I've already staked out. In the meantime, I'm simply suggesting that we should take seriously the problems with the dogmatic assertion that we can ever absolutely know we are doing the world good.

These arguments also intersect with the emphasis of this book on a deep concern for the distant future. If the correct social rate of discount were sufficiently high, uncertainty about the distant future wouldn't matter so much because, given the logic of discounting, most future consequences would cease to matter within a few decades. At low rates of discount, however, the spinning out of the future consequences of current acts is an exercise that can go on and on and on. We cannot dismiss the importance of the future simply because it is distant from us in time, and therefore we need to worry about epistemic problems all the more.

So, to proceed, I'm going to step back and consider whether epistemic problems upset the entire consequentialist framework. At the same time, I'm going to revisit some questions about Crusonia plants from earlier chapters. Might the epistemic problem and the importance of Crusonia plants have some underlying connection? I'll be returning to that question once I work through some examples of the radical uncertainty of the future.

Finding cases where consequences clearly should matter
I will focus on the example of a terrorist who brings deadly instruments of biological warfare to the United States. The pathogens are

so deadly that, if released, they would kill one million people. Of course we should try to stop the terrorist, or at least reduce his impact or probability of success, because this will save lives and also help protect the United States more generally. This should not be a controversial stance, regardless of what the correct detailed ethical and meta-ethical views might be.

Yet trying to stop the terrorist does not commit us to a very clear vision of how, exactly, an effective defense would work out in the longer run. To return to the logic explained above, stopping the terrorist will influence the broader physical world, and thus reshuffle the genetic identities behind many subsequent conceptions. That could bring about the birth of a future Genghis Khan or some worse tyrant yet, armed with more powerful weapons than Khan ever had. Even trying to stop the terrorist, with no guarantee of success, will reshape the future in similar fashion. Still, there is at least a slight chance (and maybe even a very definite chance) that stopping the attack will favor good consequences, even in the longest of runs. To put it simply, it is difficult to see a major biowarfare attack as favoring the long-term prospects of civilization on net, in expected value terms.

To be sure, there are possible scenarios in which the attack works out for the better. For instance, it might lead to a broader ban of biological weapons and thus avert a greater catastrophe in the future. Maybe so. But no rational human being would breathe a sigh of relief upon hearing that the attack succeeded. We would not, in that moment, think of the world as being on a path to salvation. More likely we would fear subsequent terror attacks of a similar nature, which might produce a new and very real gateway toward global chaos and tyranny, with adverse consequences for decades or maybe even centuries to come.

In other words, there will be certain events and consequences so significant that we will be spurred to action without much epistemic reluctance, even though we might recognize the broader uncertain-ties of such action in the very long run. Surely in some instances the upfront benefit of an action must be large enough to persuade us to pursue it.[2]

We can therefore avoid complete paralysis or sheer and absolute ag-nosticism, at least for some of our choices. No matter how high the uncertainty surrounding long-term consequences, we can take some actions to favor good consequences in the short run. It is only neces-sary that those short-run good consequences are of sufficiently large and obvious value.

The epistemic critique does not focus on the pursuit of large, upfront benefits. Instead, the articles in this philosophic literature often spec-ify very small, "squirrely" benefits. There's a reason for this, namely that those cases lend the epistemic critique greater weight. So let's look at these arguments in more detail.

James Lenman, a philosopher and a commentator in this literature, doubts the importance of consequences as a measure of right and wrong. Lenman's arguments are interesting, but I think that, properly understood, they strengthen the case for rules-based, big-picture thinking about consequences. Let's first go through Lenman's argu-ments, and then we'll return to what the whole mess might mean.[3]

Lenman presents a D-Day example in which we must choose which French beach to invade to defeat the Nazis. This is, of course, an im-

2. The economic literature on probability offers a debate about whether we can ever say we have "no idea" about the likelihood of an outcome. Under one view, we can always attach a Bayesian probability, whether explicit or implicit, to various outcomes (Caplan 1999). Even if we are very uncertain, in principle there exist betting odds that we would or would not be willing to take on a given choice. These counterfactual bets help us pin down implicit probability estimates for any imaginable outcome. Under a second view, we simply cannot assign probabilities to some events (O'Driscoll and Rizzo 1996). Those events are unique and "radically uncertain," and thus do not fit into the standard categories of probability theory. But even in these cases we still have degrees of uncertainty. I may have "no idea" about my forthcoming birthday surprise, but this uncertainty is not comparable to my "no idea" about intelligent life on other planets. Background social context will give us some expectations, even if we cannot assign definite numbers to probability forecasts. For an earlier look at the argument that we often have some idea about consequences, see Mill (1969 [1852], 180).

3. Lenman (2000) appears to favor "ethical theories for which the focus is on the character of agents and the qualities of their wills, for theories that are broadly Kantian or Aristotelian in spirit."

portant decision, with significant consequences for the outcome of the war. In the example, we must choose between two candidate beaches for the invasion, yet there is no strong military reason to favor one beach over the other. One of the two choices is likely to end up being the superior decision; we just don't know which. There is, however, a complicating factor: if we land at the northern beach, a dog will break one of its legs and suffer some pain, possibly as a result of the military action. (How about a slight sprain for the poor dog instead?) If we land at the southern beach, no canine injury occurs.

Although most plausible moral theories attach some weight to the suffering of animals, it seems that the fate of the dog's leg is not a strong reason to favor the southern beach over the northern beach, and maybe it isn't a reason at all. The matter of the dog's leg and the associated pain just seems tiny compared to what is at stake: the outcome of World War II. And so, even ex ante, we should not elevate the matter of the dog's leg into any kind of deciding position, according to Lenman, because the dog's leg will prove negligible in the final analysis. That whole argument makes some sense to me. But then Lenman concludes that we should not be so keen to judge actions in terms of their consequences at all. As you can see, this argument is one version of the epistemic critique.

The hard-line response, of course, dismisses Lenman's intuition rather than responding to it. We can imagine the extreme consequentialist crying out, "Save the dog from a broken leg, grab the gain we can see, and damn the uncertainty! The potential variance of outcomes from the invasion decision is high in any case!"

But that's not my answer. I'm willing to accept that there is something to Lenman's basic point. My reply is this: "Stop the terrorist with his biowarfare; about the dog's leg I couldn't say. Maybe Lenman is right and this D-Day case is up for debate." We are then left with the view that consequentialism is strongest when we pursue values that are high in absolute importance. You can debate where to draw the line between the biowarfare attack and the dog's leg, but once a distinction is made between cases which differ in terms of the size of the upfront costs, we have something to work with.

The use of a dog's broken leg as the relevant cost is designed to be murky. There is real merit in animal welfare arguments, but in a lot of comparisons we just don't know how much power to give them. We don't, for instance, know how to weight the welfare of dogs against the welfare of humans, so it is relatively easy for the epistemic critique to boost such uncertainty and cause us to doubt whether consequentialism is ever applicable. Focusing on the dog's leg, a relatively small and also potentially ambiguous value, gives the epistemic critique the appearance of more power than it merits.

For the sake of contrast, let's consider another invasion scenario. In this case, choosing the northern beach will result in the deaths of five hundred innocent children and choosing the southern beach won't result in any harm to civilians at all. In this case the choice is easy, because five hundred innocent lives have a consequentialist power and clarity that the dog's leg does not, even though our choice will still set off a chain of uncertain longer-run effects. There is no good reason not to choose saving five hundred innocent lives upfront, given that the initial benefit is sufficiently large.

Now let's look at some intermediate cases and see what happens. We'll find further support for the notion that a modified form of consequentialism that focuses on large benefits and costs does fine when faced with the epistemic critique.

The epistemic critique may indeed be drawing on a different moral principle altogether, a principle that pops up frequently in pluralistic approaches. Let us consider what I call the Principle of roughness:

The Principle of Roughness: Outcomes can differ in complex ways. We might make a reasoned judgment that they are roughly equal in value and we should be roughly indifferent to them. After making a small improvement to one of these outcomes, we still might not be sure which is better.

We often resort to some version of the Principle of Roughness in matters of beauty and aesthetics. Try to figure out whether Rembrandt or Velazquez was the better painter. You might judge the two as being of roughly the same quality and import, or at least decide that neither should be placed above the other. If we then discover one new sketch by Rembrandt, we don't suddenly have to conclude that he was in fact the better artist. We still can hold the two to be roughly equal in quality and importance.[4]

The Principle of Roughness may apply to many judgments of goodness. Imagine, for example, that you are comparing a new vaccination program to a program that would improve the quality of antibiotics for one group of children. These policies may be broadly equivalent in value, at least if their potential impact were sufficiently similar in magnitude. This judgment of rough equality would again survive the realization that one of the two policies was slightly better than previously thought or would cost slightly less than anticipated.

The Principle of Roughness, when it applies, implies that we should not discriminate on the basis of relatively small benefits and losses. The future changes at stake—the rest of human history being up for grabs—seem so large that relatively small changes in upfront benefits and costs, such as the dog's broken leg, do not move the initial comparison out of the category of the unclear and the blurry.

In the comparison of Rembrandt vs. Velazquez, small changes, such as finding another unpublished sketch, are overwhelmed by the high absolute totals of creativity. As for the D-Day comparison, the small

---

4. Philosophers often write of the closely related ideas of incommensurability and incomparability. On these ideas more generally, see Chang (1997, 2002). On the related concept of vagueness, see the work of Timothy Williamson, for instance "Vagueness in Reality" (2003).

change—the dog's leg—is swamped by uncertainty about consequences. In other words, the epistemic critique extends one version of the Principle of Roughness to comparisons involving uncertainty. Still, consequentialism is left standing, at least provided we are pursuing large upfront benefits, such as saving five hundred innocent lives.

Or look at it this way: anything we try to do is *floating in a sea of long-run radical uncertainty*, so to speak. Only big, important upfront goals will, in reflective equilibrium, stand above the ever-present froth and allow the comparison to be more than a very rough one. Putting too many small goals at stake simply means that our moral intuitions will end up confused, which is in fact the correct and intuitive conclusion. If there is any victim of the epistemic critique, it is the focus on small benefits and costs, but not consequentialism more generally. If we bundle appropriately and "think big" and pursue Crusonia plants, our moral intuitions will rise above the froth of long-run variance.

Purveyors of the epistemic critique might suggest that consequences should not matter very much, at least not compared to deontology or virtue ethics, given how hard they are to predict. But the better conclusion is that the froth of uncertainty should induce us to elevate the import of large benefits relative to small benefits, so as to overcome the Principle of Roughness. In other words, yet another aspect of moral theory is directing our attention toward the pursuit of Crusonia plants.

What are the practical implications of these arguments?
The arguments above have (at least) two practical implications for what we should believe, how we should believe, and how we should act. I will consider agnosticism and individual rights in turn.

How to be a good agnostic
We should be skeptical of ideologues who claim to know all of the relevant paths to making ours a better world. How can we be sure that a

favored ideology will in fact bring about good consequences? Given the radical uncertainty of the more distant future, we can't know how to achieve preferred goals with any kind of certainty over longer time horizons. Our attachment to particular means should therefore be highly tentative, highly uncertain, and radically contingent.

Our specific policy views, though we may rationally believe them to be the best available, will stand only a slight chance of being correct. They ought to stand the highest chance of being correct of all available views, but this chance will not be very high in absolute terms. Compare the choice of one's politics to betting on the team most favored to win the World Series at the beginning of the season. That team does indeed have the best chance of winning, but most of the time it does not end up being the champion. Most of the time our sports predictions are wrong, even if we are good forecasters on average. So it is with politics and policy.

Our attitudes toward others should therefore be accordingly tolerant. Imagine that your chance of being right is three percent, and your corresponding chance of being wrong is ninety-seven percent. Each opposing view, however, has only a two percent chance of being right, which of course is a bit less than your own chance of being right. Yet there are many such opposing views, so even if yours is the best, you're probably still wrong. Now imagine that your wrongness will lead to a slower rate of economic growth, a poorer future, and perhaps even the premature end of civilization (not enough science to fend off that asteroid!). That means your political views, though they are the best ones out there, will have grave negative consequences with probability .98 (one minus two percent, the latter being the chance that you are right on the details of the means-end relationships). In this setting, how confident should you really be about the details of your political beliefs? How firm should your dogmatism be about means-ends relationships? Probably not very; better to adopt a tolerant demeanor and really mean it.

As a general rule, we should not pat ourselves on the back and feel that we are on the correct side of an issue. We should choose the course that is most likely to be correct, keeping in mind that at the end of the day we are still more likely to be wrong than right. Our particular views, in politics and elsewhere, should be no more certain than our assessments of which team will win the World Series. With this attitude political posturing loses much of its fun, and indeed it ought to be viewed as disreputable or perhaps even as a sign of our own overconfident and delusional nature.

Why the case for rights is compelling, and which rights are the important ones
The epistemic critique also helps us understand why we should respect individual rights rather than overturning them in favor of better consequences. They also help us outline the limits of those individual rights.

Let us consider, for instance, the right of an innocent baby not to be murdered. Let's say you believe in such a right, as I do, but you are then presented with a counterexample in which killing that innocent baby will, in the short run, raise national income by $5 billion. Normally, economists would value a life at much less than $5 billion; they'd typically value it in the neighborhood of $5 million, which is a big difference. Yet in this instance it is wrong to set up the comparison as "baby's life vs. $5 billion" and then have to choose. The correct comparison is "baby's life vs. a froth of massive uncertainty with a gain of $5 billion tossed in as one element of that froth." When phrased that way, it is easier to side with preventing the murder of the baby. There is even a good chance—albeit a less than fifty percent chance—that stopping the murder of the baby will be good for GDP, too.

In other words, rights rarely conflict with consequences in the simple ways set out by philosophical thought experiments. We can therefore shift the way we think about radical uncertainty and consequences. Rather than letting it paralyze us, we can think of radical uncertainty as giving us the freedom to act morally, without the fear that we are engaging in consequentialist destruction.

We can also see this radical uncertainty as supporting a new enchantment with human life and choice; we can accept that most or all of our actions will have consequences we cannot possibly predict. On average these consequences will be positive, just as average economic growth is positive, but we will always wonder about the future consequences we have set in motion. We will wonder about our strange and almost magical powers in this regard.

For all the confusion we might feel about the marginal product of an individual act, this is also an empowering notion, and it relates to the idea that all fruitful societies are based on some notion of faith. In this case we can hold onto our faith in doing the right thing—and indeed doing the right thing for its own sake—without being brutally beaten back by the fear that we are bringing about some sort of consequentialist disaster.

Now let's consider another crazy philosophical thought experiment: either we murder a specified baby, or aliens from Alpha Centauri will destroy the entire Earth. Here we have more room to be what is called a rights consequentialist. Murdering the one baby is wrong, but if we don't do it, even more babies will be murdered—many millions more, in fact. On one side of the equation, we have "murder one baby." On the other side of the equation, we have "all babies get murdered, everything on Earth is lost, and, since human life on Earth ends, no more Crusonia plants, no significant froth of uncertainty to follow."

It is possible to see why we would opt to kill the baby in this case. For one thing, the cost of not murdering the baby is now much higher. For another—and this is significant—if the entire world ends, there is no residual uncertainty about what will happen next. We should pursue the better consequences, and there is no remaining froth of uncertainty to justify sticking with the rights of the individual baby. And in that sense, the notion of rights postulated here is not strictly absolute against all possible external consequences that philosophers might dream up. Still, most or all of the hypothetical examples in which rights should be violated are not very relevant to the real-world choices we have had to face so far.

To be sure, we do not know exactly where this comparison should end and at what point the case for murdering an innocent baby looks strong. What if the choice is murdering one baby or aliens will destroy only the nation of Nepal? The number of lives affected by the alien threat could be made larger or smaller until the rights theorist cries uncle. We don't know exactly where to draw that line. You can think of this as one of the weaknesses of the rights theory I am putting forward. Still, this leaves us with a rights theory in which rights are indeed absolute, at least provided the examples we consider match some very basic facts about the real world, for instance the existence of Crusonia plants and the froth of consequentialist uncertainty.

Using this understanding of the epistemic problem, we can also see some further evidence for why "lifeboat ethics" might differ from our more usual and more practical ethical recommendations. I define lifeboat ethics as the ethics which should govern as the end of the world—or the end of some sufficiently segmented part of the world—approaches. People in a (not-to-be-rescued) lifeboat cannot look forward to great improvements in their future welfare or much economic growth. The sharks are circling and supplies of food and water will run out. By design, the lifeboat in this example is not connected to the broader froth of uncertainty in the world at large.

So what does that mean? In lifeboat settings, the benefits at stake will typically be small precisely because lifeboats, even the relatively large ones, are small. Rights therefore acquire greater force, in relative terms. No matter what you do, you can't produce large social benefits in lifeboat examples, so there is a stronger case to be made for simply doing the right thing. Don't toss the weak guy overboard or cook his flesh; it is the wrong thing to do, and there is only so much to be gained from it. Making an omelette may require the breaking of some eggs, but here the omelette is small, and not very tasty besides, so I say leave those eggs intact. Once again, the case for human rights is stronger than it appears at first.

Conclusion

Some of my arguments have concerned the theme of distance. I have claimed that the inhabitants of the future are less distant from us, in moral terms, than many other views would indicate. Therefore, we should take more seriously the implications of our choices for that future.

That greater concern for the future induces us to rethink a variety of moral questions, including the importance of economic growth and the best kinds of redistribution, and it makes the stability of social systems a higher priority, among other considerations. The previous chapter on agnosticism and radical uncertainty made an additional argument for being willing to think big. If our values are to rise in importance above the froth of long-run uncertainty about the effects of our actions, we must look to relatively large and important values. This returns us to a place where Crusonia plants reign supreme and sustainable economic growth is all-important.

Here is my short, three-point summary of where these arguments have brought us:

First, believing in the overriding importance of sustained economic growth is more than philosophically tenable. Indeed, it may be philosophically imperative. We should pursue large rather than small benefits, and we should have a deep concern for the more distant future rather than discounting it exponentially. Our working standard for evaluating choices should be to increase sustainable economic growth, because those choices overcome aggregation problems and are decisively good. That provides us with a broad quantitative proxy for the long-run development of human civilization, and it constitutes one means of finding and promoting comoving plural values.

Second, there is plenty of room for our morality, including our political morality, to be strict and based in the notion of rules and rights. We should subject ourselves to the constraint of respecting human rights, noting that only semi-absolute human rights will be strong enough to place any constraint on pursuing the benefits of a higher rate of sustainable economic growth.

At the end of this tunnel we do not have the "Best Ethical Theory," as a philosopher might wish to derive, but rather some good decision-making rules to live by, as well as some standards for how we might imagine a much brighter future.

To be sure, I have made no attempt to prove the absolute existence of rights. But once we start thinking in terms of big, comprehensive changes, a belief in rights fits in quite naturally. We have some rules for what to do—maximize sustainable growth—and other rules—rights—which place some constraints on those choices. In other words, the lower-order rules exist within the confines of higher-order rules, namely respecting human rights. We should stick to our chosen priorities and our chosen rules rigidly. Rather than rights and consequentialist considerations representing warring or contrasting approaches to philosophy, the door is open for consilience and compatibilism to reign, all within a rules-nested approach to thinking about both the rights-based and the practical, consequentialist sides of the equation.

We need not defend such rules-based perspectives on the grounds that they are a highly practical "noble lie." It is nice to see the practical benefits of rules recognized, but the noble lie approach is too cynical. It assumes that rules are philosophically weak to begin with when they are not. So rather than viewing belief in strict rules as a noble lie, view it as a very important noble truth.

On the purely practical side, it is unlikely that democratic real-world decision-makers will think too big. The nature of politics is more likely to produce too much small fry than too little. Policymakers often make decisions on a day-to-day, case-by-case basis, simply hoping to survive the next election cycle. I don't mean that as a cynical criticism of human nature; rather, it is an implication of political competition within relatively short electoral cycles relative to the time horizons over which policy matters. (The U.S. House of Representatives has a two-year voting cycle for policies which may have effects over twenty or thirty years, or, in the case of environmental policies, longer still.) That is one reason why our politics makes as many mistakes as it does. So, from a purely pragmatic or consequentialist point of view, there is an additional argument to be made for imagining our political choices in terms of broader bundles of choices and rules, at least provided we get the rules right.

Third, we should be very cautious in our attitudes about specific policies. Even if we succeed in taking true aim at what we think are the best courses of action, the chance that we are right on the specifics— even if the chance is as high as possible—is still not very high. It's like trying to guess at the origin of the universe. The best you can do is to pick what you think is right at 1.05 percent certainty, rather than siding with what you think is right at 1.03 percent. Most likely you're wrong, even if others are likely to be even more wrong than you are, and thus your attitude should be correspondingly modest in the epistemic sense.

For some more concrete recommendations, I'll suggest the following:

a. Policy should be more forward-looking and more concerned about the more distant future.

b. Governments should place a much higher priority on investment than is currently the case, in both the private sector and the public sector. Relative to what we should be doing, we are currently living in an investment drought.

c. Policy should be more concerned with economic growth, properly specified, and policy discussion should pay less heed to other values. And yes, that means your favorite value gets downgraded too. No exceptions, except of course for the semi-absolute human rights.

d. We should be more concerned with the fragility of our civilization.

    The possibility of historical pessimism stands as a challenge to this entire approach, because in that view the future is dim no matter what, and there may not be a more distant future we can look toward in order to resolve the aggregation dilemmas involved in making decisions that affect so many human beings.

e. We should be more charitable on the whole, but we are not obliged to give away all of our wealth. We do have an obligation to work hard, save, invest, and fulfill our human potential, and we should take these obligations very seriously.

f. We can embrace much of common sense morality with the knowledge that it is not inconsistent with a deeper ethical theory. Common sense morality can also be reconciled with many of the normative recommendations which emerge from a more impersonal and consequentialist framework.

g. When it comes to most "small" policies affecting the present and the near-present only, we should be agnostic, because we cannot overcome aggregation problems to render a defensible judgment. The main exceptions here are the small number of policies which benefit virtually everybody.

The utopian vision

My utopian political vision is a society that follows these principles. That means a society that lets individuality, happiness, and autonomy flower to their maximum extent. I don't expect something so good to actually come about, but it is nonetheless a vision to live by and one to use when defining one's personal and political philosophy. And for smaller subsets of political issues, especially those which are so narrow that they would not affect sustainable economic growth, there is plenty of room for coexisting visions, political and otherwise. There is a significant open-ended aspect to this approach, and it represents one building block of political thought rather than a closed system that answers or addresses every possible question. You can adopt this perspective without having to give up all of your other micro-visions for a better political and social order.

That all said, most normative work is connected to some gut-level intuition, and this exposition is no exception. I have the feeling—and yes, I am willing to describe it as such—that we should look more than a bit beyond our currently perceived constraints. It is easy enough to perform the obviously beneficial small tasks; the most important policy advice should not always feel comfortable or practical.

We should strive to significantly augment future human well-being over long spans of time. As we struggle for great achievements, we will encounter many incidental costs and obstacles along the way. We are not certain how much weight we should attach to these costs, just as we were not sure how to value the dog's broken leg in the D-Day example in chapter five, given the high uncertainty associated with our choices. But these incidental costs—and benefits—are probably less important than we think. They should be less of an obstacle to our attempts to improve our civilization and render it more durable.

When thinking about policy, I often have a little voice inside my head that says, "Let's just worry about making some small improvement today. Grand schemes come to naught. What is the future, anyway? Aren't current improvements, however small, hard enough to implement? Let us be supreme pragmatists and focus only on the here and now. That is the best we can do for the future, in any case. The future can take care of itself. Let us drop our fantasies."

But then I think again, and I realize that I am engaging in a comfortable form of self-deception. I know that we as human beings are biologically programmed to respond to immediate stimuli and the near term at the expense of the future. Many of us do not plan far enough ahead or save enough for our retirements. Sufficiently thirsty individuals will drink salt water out of desperation, even if it lessens their chances of survival. So we cannot always trust our innate programming and response mechanisms. These mechanisms may have been adaptive in hunter-gatherer societies, but they are suddenly more costly in a flourishing civilization with large-scale political institutions, persistent long-run problems, and the ability to generate sustained and compounding economic growth.

I would therefore like to be more suspicious of our little voice in favor of supreme short-run pragmatism. I wish to suggest that it is a vice, the thinking man's equivalent of the savage's short-run gratification. It is our latest adaptive mechanism for feeling good about ourselves, at the expense of letting Rome burn. I suggest that we should instead turn our political energies to thinking about the long-run fortunes of our civilization. That means focusing on the future of freedom, wealth, science, and healthy, well-functioning institutions governed by rules and rights.

I end this book by reiterating some core claims. Our civilization carries many wonderful plural values. Preserving and extending those values through time should be our priority. Sustainable economic growth elevates living standards and human welfare, and delivers other plural values. The case for a good society, appropriately specified, is sound, and it does not fall prey to the usual problems of utilitarianism or consequentialism. It is permissible to believe in absolute or near-absolute human rights. We can be, and must be, partially utopian in our personal and political commitments. We should not be afraid to think in terms of the big picture, rather than evaluating everything on a case-by-case basis. We should be deeply skeptical of particular instrumental views of what is likely to promote the good.

We still do not have the Best Ethical Theory. But we should live our lives to the fullest, knowing that common sense morality has a deep connection to what is truly right.

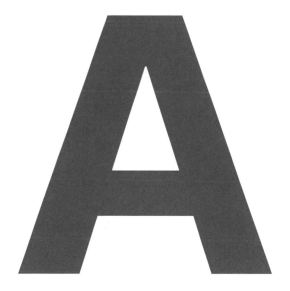

Appendix A—Some optional mathematics and remarks on a few metrics

Mathematically, we can formalize our concern for the future in a few ways. The simplest method postulates a strict zero discounting of utility. In mathematical terms, it looks like this:

$$(1) \quad SW = \Sigma \, U \, (a^t)$$

An ethics based on that equation would mean basic neutrality for utilities across time. No person's well-being would count for less simply because of its temporal distance.[1]

Another approach builds on the "Golden Rule" in the economic theory of capital. The Golden Rule tells us to choose the highest sustainable path of utility or consumption over time. Mathematically, it looks like this:

$$(2) \quad Max: \, lim \, U \, (a^t)$$

That is, we should maximize a steady state value—in this case, Wealth Plus—over an indefinite time horizon.[2]

I sympathize with both zero discounting of well-being and the Golden Rule. And under a variety of technical conditions, the two principles will imply the same choices across all comparisons.[3] But there is another approach to comparing current and future values. An explicitly zero rate of discount would require that a future interest always receives equal consideration to a current interest. Whether or not this conclusion fits our moral intuitions, it sounds like a very strong claim, especially with that word "always." As for the Golden Rule, the prop-

1. Cowen (1992) tries to axiomatize this approach.

2. For early presentations of the Golden Rule, see Ramsey (1928), Phelps (1961), and Meade (1962). The "Green" Golden Rule pays closer attention to resource exhaustibility but embodies the same basic principles; see Beltratti, Chichilnisky, and Heal (1993) and Heal (1998).

3. Heal (1998, 110-111) discusses these conditions. For a version of an overtaking axiom, but more general and without the same continuity requirements, see Basu and Mitra (2007); see also Banerjee (2006) for an analysis of related ideas. For a look at related philosophical issues, see Vallentyne (1993, 1995) and Vallentyne and Kagan (1997).

erties of the mathematics make it hard to generalize beyond the infinite horizon case.

As a modification of these approaches, the overtaking criterion is a more modest rule of thumb for present/future trade-offs. We should always be willing to give up a discrete benefit today if in return we can create a sufficiently long string of well-being increases for the future. Yet the criterion does not specify any single numerical or universally applicable discount rate. We can write the following:

The Overtaking Criterion: A sequence $g^{\infty} = (b^1, b^2, ...)$ is preferred to $h^{\infty} = (a^1, a^2, ...)$ if one sequence, at some point in time, remains systematically higher than the other. For instance, compare the two sequences:

(a)   *3, 3, 4, 4, 5, 6, 6, 6, 6, 6, 6, 6, 6*...

(b)   *4, 4, 5, 5, 5, 5, 5, 5, 5, 5, 5, 5*...

By design, sequence (a) will continue with sixes, and sequence (b) will continue with fives. Using the overtaking criterion, (a) is better than (b), even though (b) brings higher well-being in the first few periods. Again, I am thinking of these numbers as corresponding to what I call Wealth Plus.

Similarly, the overtaking criterion will prefer (c) to (d) for:

(c)   *3, 3, 7, 8, 9, 10, 11, 12, 13, 14*...

(d)   *4, 4, 6, 7, 8, 9, 10, 11, 12, 13*...

As written, this assumes that each element in each sequence continues to rise by one.

I do not require the superimposition of an infinite time horizon for the overtaking criterion to make sense. Instead, we can prefer (a) to

(b) and (c) to (d) if the relevant time horizon is long enough for one sequence to be obviously welfare-dominating over the other. Quite simply, if (a) beats (b) for a few hundred years, I am happy to sign off on preferring (a). We can also add Pareto principles to the overtaking criterion so that if one sequence has some unambiguously higher values along the way, it is better even if it does not overtake the other for all later periods of time, but rather remains equal to it.[4]

Low rates of discount, as expressed through this variety of mathematical assumptions, might appear to give the future too much weight relative to the present. But there are deep empirical reasons why the present will not fade into irrelevance in our decisions. Economic growth is a cumulative process with causal relationships between the variables at the beginning of growth and at the later stages of growth. This means that—usually—the best way to satisfy the overtaking criterion is to put the present in a good position to build for the future. Put another way, economic growth requires that we invest in healthy institutions, which means doing some good things for the here and now, too.[5]

Cyclic theories of society, as found in some of the classic thinkers, such as Montesquieu and Vico, would make it difficult to apply an overtaking criterion in a useful way. Assume, for instance, that successful societies become infected by hubris and then self-destruct as a consequence of their earlier success. Furthermore, it might be the fallen societies which rise from the ashes and go on to achieve greater glories. In this case, a higher sequence in one period would mean, on average, systematically lower sequences in later future periods. Systematic overtaking would never hold. That said, while there may

---

4. Chichilnisky (1997) suggests a modified version of the overtaking criterion that does not force the present time period to count for nothing. We could entertain such an alternative if in fact we did face an infinite time horizon and a "dictatorship of the future" problem. Note that with an infinite horizon, the Overtaking Criterion will fail to satisfy certain axioms of intergenerational equity, such as anonymity or indifference across labeling decisions. On the difficulties of satisfying all reasonable axioms in an infinite horizon setting, see for instance Fleurbaey and Michel (2003) and Sakai (2003). Asheim, Buchholz, and Tungodden (2001) respond to some charges of this kind. On the postulates of stationarity and independence, see Koopmans (1960). Bostrom (2011) considers some philosophical and mathematical issues within an infinite horizon framework.

5. On the fundamentally cooperative nature of the intergenerational problem, see Heath (2013). For an interesting look at sustainable generational exchange over time, see Rangel (2000).

be some degree of catch-up at play, there is not much systematic evidence that today's losers become tomorrow's winners. If you're trying to predict absolute levels of future prosperity, you're generally well advised to bet on the previous winners, for reasons discussed in chapter three.[6]

Comparison with gamma discounting

There is another way to derive relatively low discount factors, and that is to consider models in which the discount factor changes over time.[7] The way that expected value calculations work, mathematically, is that the lowest discount rate will have a relatively high contribution to the final assessment of an outcome. This stems from the literature on what is known as gamma discounting, and it leads to results broadly consistent with a deep concern for the distant future.

Here is a simple way to think about the logic: say there is an equal chance that the relevant interest rate will be either one percent or five percent. The value of one dollar in one hundred years is 36.9 cents at a one percent discount rate but only 0.76 cents at a discount rate of five percent. Due to the convexity of returns, the average or expected value discount rate is below two percent, because that is the rate at which you would get 36.9 + 0.76 divided by two as an expected payoff. It is wrong to average the discount rates themselves, for instance by taking 1 + 5 = 6 and then dividing by two to get an average of three percent. The averaging is applied to the payoffs, and that gives the lower discount rates a greater influence over the expected values overall.[8]

So the lower discount rates have greater weight for determining the assessment of distant future values. This does not exactly mirror the overtaking criterion, but it does increase its plausibility by favoring a relatively low discount rate.[9]

6. On the convergence issue, see for instance Pritchett (1997) and also Comin, Easterly, and Gong (2010).

7. See Weitzman (1998, 2012), and also Farmer and Geanakoplos (2009) and Arrow et al. (2014).

8. See Posner (2004, 153–154) and also Weitzman (2001, 260).

Our actual behavior sometimes reflects a version of gamma discounting. On questionnaires, for instance, many people will suggest that the present is more important than forty years hence, but that eventually further distances of time should cease to matter very much. In this view, what happens four hundred years from now is not much less important than what happens three hundred years from now, even though the application of strict exponential discounting would suggest otherwise.[10]

My arguments are consistent with the spirit of gamma discounting, but I have chosen a slightly different direction, as discussed above. Gamma discounting still implies that we can choose a single correct (non-zero) number or set of numbers for the long-term rate of discount. If such rates are positive, we still face the possibility that a single life today will be worth more than continued world survival, provided we choose a long enough time horizon for the comparison. For most practical issues, such problems are unlikely to arise, but I find this conclusion morally counterintuitive nonetheless. Alternatively, we might choose a zero rate for the latter years of our gamma discounting comparisons, in which case we will move closer to the overtaking criterion.

9. See Weitzman (2001, 260).

10. See for instance Price (1993) and Weitzman (2001) for versions of this view. Leahy (2000) argues that standard techniques measure how much a current agent cares about his future self, when we could just as well ask how much a future self would care about the current self. Adjusting for this discrepancy could also cause us to choose lower discount rates and hold greater concern for the distant future.

Appendix B—Animal welfare and Derek Parfit's repugnant conclusion

Before closing, I'd like to offer a few remarks on the problem that ini-
tially drew my attention to rational choice ethics, namely Derek
Parfit's repugnant conclusion. I first read Parfit's work in 1984, and
I've been thinking about it ever since. I haven't solved or refuted his
repugnant conclusion, but given the framework of these arguments,
I'll sum up my thinking and look at why the repugnant conclusion
still represents a hole in some of these arguments. By the way, if you
don't like reasoning from "absurd" moral counterfactuals, you can
stop reading right now.

Parfit's repugnant conclusion compares two population scenarios.
The first outcome has a very large, very fulfilled, and very happy population. The world also has many ideal goods, such as beauty, virtue,
and justice. The second outcome has a much larger population but
few, if any, ideal goods. Parfit asks us to conceive of a world of "Muzak and potatoes." Nonetheless, the lives in this scenario are still
worth living, although perhaps by only the tiniest of margins. Parfit
points out that if the population of the second scenario is large
enough, the second scenario could welfare-dominate the first. No
matter how good we make the first world, quantity can weigh in on
the side of the second.[1]

Few people would regard the second scenario—a world of Muzak and
potatoes—as better than the first. Yet it is surprisingly difficult to find
a welfare algorithm that avoids the endorsement of sheer numbers
per se. Many of the attempts to cut off an endorsement of the second
scenario fall prey to further philosophic counterexamples.[2]

Parfit's statement of the repugnant conclusion reads as follows: "The
Repugnant Conclusion. For any possible population of at least ten
billion people, all with a very high quality of life, there must be some

1. See Parfit (1984, 1986).

2. Cowen (1996) surveys some of the different options, such as capping the importance of numbers
or capping the importance of total utility. See also Cowen (2005).

much larger imaginable population, whose existence, if other things were equal, would be better, even though its members have lives that are barely worth living."[3]

I'm not going to work through all of the different attempts to solve (or state) this conundrum, as entire books have been devoted to that purpose. For my purposes, it suffices to note that most people refuse to endorse the repugnant conclusion because they feel that very small utilities, no matter how large in number, ought not to add up to something with great moral significance. That is, they downgrade the very small utilities that comprise the lives of Muzak and potatoes.

I've focused on Wealth Plus as a foundational concept for a Crusonia plant around which we can build a moral theory. I've found, I think, one such Crusonia plant, but I haven't offered any argument that this is our only Crusonia plant. I've picked a Crusonia plant from the lives of human beings as we know them, namely lives full of ideal goods whose richness extends well beyond the consumption of Muzak and potatoes. Parfit's repugnant conclusion can be read as depicting the results of another Crusonia plant consisting of a very, very long sequence of "Muzak and potatoes" lives. It is easy enough to flesh out Parfit's scenario and have these Muzak and potatoes lives be numerous because they are self-reproducing and go on for a very long time.

When I think about the repugnant conclusion in a very literal fashion, I'm not sure those Muzak and potatoes lives are well described by comparing them to human lives as we know them. Even in the world's poorest countries, people have rich human relations and very moving and beautiful cultures. Maybe those Muzak and potatoes lives are better described by a comparison with (some) non-human animals. That is, there are animals whose lives are worth living, even though they don't have most of the goods we associate with flourishing and more complex human lives. Why should we choose flourishing and more complex human lives over a larger number of slightly happy animal lives? Might we not consider voluntarily extinguishing the human race to make more room for a greater number of non-human animals?

In other words, once we consider non-human lives, there are multiple competing Crusonia plants. I do not and cannot, within this framework, give you any reason for choosing the Crusonia plant of human lives as we know them rather than a Crusonia plant drawn from other realms of nature. I can only say that, for practical purposes, we have to work with the Crusonia plant before us, which is very much centered on the rich, plural vision for human lives as we know them in their excellence.

For similar reasons, the arguments of this book do not and cannot resolve long-standing disputes over animal welfare and animal rights. I do personally have considerable sympathy for the view that we should treat non-human animals better than we do now. But the rights of animals, at least non-domesticated animals, belong to a different Crusonia plant from the one we are considering. Nothing within my framework, as presented here, will resolve those debates.

You may recall that some frameworks, such as contractarianism, imply that animal welfare issues stand outside of the mainstream discourse of ethics because we have not and cannot form agreements, even hypothetical ones, with (non-domesticable) animals. There is no bargaining with a starling, even though starlings appear to be much smarter than we once thought. My reasons for excluding animals from the argument are different, and have little to do with consent or hypothetical consent.

One implication of this argument is that we will not have an easy way of circumventing aggregation problems when it comes to animal welfare issues because there is—domesticable animals aside—no common Crusonia plant. This also explains why some of the more convincing treatments of animal welfare are not those of the utilitarians but rather of the Christian commentators on animal welfare, such as Matthew Scully and his excellent book *Dominion: The Power of Man, the Suffering of Animals, and the Call to Mercy*. For Christian thinkers, but not utilitarians, it is natural to see animal welfare as falling under a separate dominion, but still deserving of our mercy, which comes relatively close to the position I am outlining in this book.

So Parfit's conundrum is likely insoluble in some central ways, just as we do not have a comprehensive moral theory for weighing the interests of humans and bats, or humans and alien beings from another planet. Moral judgments occur within some kind of cone of value, and we must look for cones which allow aggregation problems to be overcome. Such cones are by no means available for every problem we might face, lifeboat situations included.

Perhaps these remarks will disappoint those who expect a moral theory to resolve Parfit's dilemmas. But we can take comfort in having classified them into a broader and better-known—though still insoluble—set of dilemmas. But within the moral cones we do have, and using those Crusonia plants we do understand, I say full steam ahead.

References

Acemoglu, Daron, Simon Johnson, and James A. Robinson. 2001. "The Colonial Origins of Comparative Development: An Empirical Investigation." *American Economic Review* 91, no. 5: 1369-1401.

Acemoglu, Daron, Simon Johnson, and James A. Robinson. 2002. "Reversal of Fortune: Geography and Institutions in the Making of the Modern World Income Distribution." *Quarterly Journal of Economics* 117, no. 4: 1231-94.

Acemoglu, Daron, Simon Johnson, and James A. Robinson. 2005. "Institutions as a Fundamental Cause of Long-Run Growth." *In Handbook of Economic Growth, Volume 1A*, edited by Philippe Aghion and Steven N. Durlauf, 385-472. Elsevier.

Alesina, Alberto, and Dani Rodrik. 1994. "Distributive Politics and Economic Growth." *Quarterly Journal of Economics* 109: 465-490.

Alexander, Peter, and Roger Gill, eds. 1984. *Utopias*. London: Duckworth.

Archer, John. 2001. "Grief from an Evolutionary Perspective." In *Handbook of Bereavement Research: Consequences, Coping, and Care*, edited by Margaret S. Stroebe, Robert O. Hansson, and Wolfgang Stroebe, 263-283. Washington, D.C.: American Psychological Association.

Argyle, M. 1999. "Causes and Correlates of Happiness." In *Well-Being: The Foundations of Hedonic Psychology*, edited by Daniel Kahneman, Edward Diener, and Nelson Schwarz. New York: Russell Sage Foundation.

Arrow, Kenneth J., Edward Leamer, Howard Schuman, and Robert Solow. 1994. "Comments of Proposed NOAA Scope Test." Appendix D of *Comments of Proposed NOAA/DOI Regulations on Natural Resource Damage Assessment*. U.S. Environmental Protection Agency.

Arrow, Kenneth J., Maureen L. Cropper, Christian Gollier, Ben Groom, Geoffrey M. Heal, Richard G. Newell, William D. Nordhaus, Robert S. Pindyck, William A. Pizer, Paul R. Portney, Thomas Sterner, Richard S.J. Tol, and Martin L. Weitzman. 2014. "Should Governments Use a Declining Discount Rate in Project Analysis?" *Review of Environmental Economics and Policy* 8, no. 2 (Summer): 145–163.

Asheim, Geir B., Wolfgang Buchholz, and Bertil Tungodden. 2001. "Justifying Sustainability." *Journal of Environmental Economics and Management* 41: 252–268.

Banerjee, Kuntal. 2006. "On the Extension of the Utilitarian and Suppes–Sen Social Welfare Relations to Infinite Utility Streams." *Social Choice and Welfare* 27, no. 2: 327–339.

Barro, Robert J. 1991. "Economic Growth in a Cross Section of Countries." *Quarterly Journal of Economics* 106, no. 2 (May): 407–443.

Basu, Kaushik, and Tapan Mitra. 2007. "Utilitarianism for Infinite Utility Streams: A New Welfare Criterion and Its Axiomatic Characterization." *Journal of Economic Theory* 133 (March): 350–373.

Becker, Gary S., Tomas J. Philipson, and Rodrigo R. Soares. 2005. "The Quantity and Quality of Life and the Evolution of World Inequality." *American Economic Review* 95, no. 1 (March): 277–291.

Beckerman, Wilfred. 1996. *Green-Colored Glasses: Environmentalism Reconsidered*. Washington, D.C.: Cato Institute.

Beltratti, Andrea, Graciela Chichilnisky, and Geoffrey Heal. 1993. "Sustainable Growth and the Green Golden Rule." NBER Working Paper No. 4430.

Blanchflower, David G., and Andrew J. Oswald. 2000. "Is the UK Moving Up the International Well-being Rankings?" Working Paper.

Borjas, George J. 1998. "The Economic Progress of Immigrants." NBER Working Paper No. 6506.

Bostrom, Nick. 2011. "Infinite Ethics." *Analysis and Metaphysics* 10: 9–59.

Bradbury, Ray. 1980. "A Sound of Thunder." In *The Stories of Ray Bradbury*. New York: Knopf.

Brandt, Richard, 1963. "Toward a Credible Theory of Utilitarianism." In *Morality and the Language of Conduct*, edited by H.N. Castaneda and G. Nakhnikian, 107–143. Detroit: Wayne State University Press.

Brennan, Geoffrey. 2007. "Discounting the Future, Yet Again." *Politics, Philosophy, and Economics* 6: 259–284.

Brennan, Geoffrey, and James M. Buchanan. 2000. *The Reason of Rules*. Indianapolis: The Liberty Fund.

Brickman, Philip, Dan Coates, and Ronnie Janoff-Bulman. 1978. "Lottery Winners and Accident Victims: Is Happiness Relative?" *Journal of Personality and Social Psychology* 36, no. 8: 917–927.

Broome, John. 1978. "Trying to Value a Life." *Journal of Public Economics* 9: 91–100.

Broome, John. 1982. "Uncertainty in Welfare Economics, and the Value of Life." In *The Value of Life and Safety*, edited by M.W. Jones-Lee. North-Holland Publishing Company.

Broome, John. 1994. "Discounting and Welfare." *Philosophy and Public Affairs* 23, no. 2 (Spring): 128–156.

Brown, Campbell. 2011. "Consequentialize This." *Ethics* 121, no. 4 (July): 749–771.

Buchanan, James M. "Politics Without Romance." 1984. In *The Theory of Public Choice II*, edited by J.M. Buchanan and Robert D. Tollison. Ann Arbor: University Press.

Buchanan, James M., and Roger L. Faith. 1979. "Trying Again to Value a Life." *Journal of Public Economics* 2: 245–248.

Bulman, Ronnie J., and Camille B. Wortman. 1977. "Attributions of Blame and Coping in the 'Real World': Severe Accident Victims React to Their Lot." *Journal of Personality and Social Psychology* 35, no. 5: 351–363.

Burch-Brown, Joanna M. 2014. "Clues for Consequentialists." *Utilitas* 26, no. 1 (March): 105–119.

Caplan, Bryan. 1999. "The Austrian Search for Realistic Foundations." *Southern Economic Journal* 65, no. 4 (April): 823–838.

Caplin, Andrew, and John Leahy. 2000. "The Social Discount Rate." NBER Working Paper No. 7983.

Castillo, Marco, Paul J. Ferraro, Jeffrey L. Jordan, and Petrie Ragan. 2011. "The Today and Tomorrow of Kids: Time Preferences and Educational Outcomes of Children." *Journal of Public Economics* 95, no. 11–12: 1377–1385.

Chang, Ruth, ed. 1997. *Incommensurability, Incomparability, and Practical Reason*. Cambridge: Harvard University Press.

Chang, Ruth. 2002. "The Possibility of Parity." *Ethics* 112 (July): 659–688.

Chichilnisky, Graciela. 1997. "What is Sustainable Development?" *Land Economics* 73, no. 4 (November): 467–491.

Chipman, John S., and James C. Moore. 1978. "The New Welfare Economics 1939–1974." *International Economic Review* 19, no. 3 (October): 547–584.

Clark, Kenneth. 1969. *Civilization*. New York: Harper & Row.

Comin, Diego, William Easterly, and Erick Gong. 2010. "Was the Wealth of Nations Determined in 1000 B.C.?" *American Economic Journal: Macroeconomics* 2, no. 3: 65–97.

Cowen, Tyler. 1992. "Consequentialism Implies a Zero Intergenerational Rate of Discount." In *Philosophy, Politics, and Society: Volume 6, Justice Between Age Groups and Generations*, edited by Peter Laslett and James Fishkin, 162–168.
Yale University Press.

Cowen, Tyler. 1996. "What Do We Learn from the Repugnant Conclusion?" *Ethics* 106: 754–775.

Cowen, Tyler. 1997. "Discounting and Restitution." *Philosophy and Public Affairs* 26, no. 2 (April): 168–185.

Cowen, Tyler. 1998. In *Praise of Commercial Culture*. Cambridge: Harvard University Press.

Cowen, Tyler. 2004. "Policy Implications of Zero Discounting: An Exploration of Politics and Morality." *Social Philosophy and Policy* 21, no. 1: 121–140.

Cowen, Tyler. 2006. "The Epistemic Problem Does Not Refute Consequentialism." *Utilitas* 18, no. 4: 383–399.

Cowen, Tyler. 2005. "Resolving the Repugnant Conclusion." In *The Repugnant Conclusion: Essays on Population Ethics*, edited by J. Ryberg and T. Tannsjo, 81–98. Dordrecht: Kluwer Academic Publishers.

Cowen, Tyler. 2007. "Caring About the Distant Future: Why It Matters and What It Means." *The University of Chicago Law Review* (Winter): 5–40.

Cowen, Tyler. 2011. "Rule Consequentialism Makes Sense After All." *Social Philosophy and Policy* 28, no. 2 (July): 212–231.

Cowen, Tyler, and Derek Parfit. 1992. "Against the Social Discount Rate." In *Philosophy, Politics, and Society: Volume 6*, edited by Peter Laslett and James Fishkin, 144–161. New Haven: Yale University Press.

Cowley, Robert, Stephen E. Ambrose, and David McCullough. 2000. ***"What If?"*** *The World's Foremost Military Historians Imagine What Might Have Been*. Berkley Publishing Group.

Crowder, George. 2002. *Liberalism & Value Pluralism*. London: Continuum.

Deaton, Angus. 2007. "Income, Aging, Health, and Well-Being Around the World: Evidence from the Gallup World Poll." NBER Working Paper No. 13317.

Diener, Ed. 1984. "Subjective Well-Being." *Psychological Bulletin* 95: 542–575.

De Jouvenel, Bertrand. 1965. "Utopia for Practical Purposes." In *Utopias and Utopian Thought*, edited by Frank E. Manuel, 219–235. Boston: Beacon Press.

DeLong, Bradford J. 2009. "Lecture 2: Slow Growth and Poverty in the North Atlantic, 1800–1870." Unpublished paper.

Demsetz, Harold. 1969. "Information and Efficiency: Another Viewpoint." *Journal of Law and Economics* 12, no. 1: 1–22.

Diamond, Jared. 2005. *Collapse: How Societies Choose to Fail or Succeed*. New York: Penguin Group.

Diener, Edward, and Shigehiro Oishi. 2000. "Money and Happiness: Income and Subjective Well-Being Across Nations." In *Culture and Subjective Well-Being*, edited by E. Diener and E. M. Suh, 185–218. Cambridge: MIT Press.

Dollar, David, and Aart Kraay. 2000. "Growth Is Good for the Poor." World Bank Working Paper.

Dorsey, Dale. 2012. "Consequentialism, Metaphysical Realism, and the Argument from Cluelessness." *The Philosophical Quarterly* 246, no. 62 (January): 48–70.

Dryregov, Atle. 1990. "Crisis Intervention Following the Loss of an Infant Child." *Bereavement Care* 9: 32–36.

Dworkin, Ronald. 1980. "Is Wealth a Value?" *The Journal of Legal Studies* 9, no. 2: 191–226.

Easterlin, Richard A. 1995. "Will Raising the Incomes of All Increase the Happiness of All?" *Journal of Economic Behavior and Organization* 27: 35–47.

Easterly, William, and Sergio Rebelo. 1993. "Fiscal Policy and Economic Growth." *Journal of Monetary Economics* 32, no. 3: 417–58.

Epstein, Richard. 1997. *Simple Rules for a Complex World*. Cambridge: Harvard University Press.

Farmer, J. Doyne, and John Geanakoplos. 2009. "Hyperbolic Discounting Is Rational: Valuing the Far Future with Uncertain Discount Rates." Cowles Foundation Discussion Paper No. 1719.

Feldman, Fred. 1997. *Utilitarianism, Hedonism, and Desert*. Cambridge: Cambridge University Press.

Fernandez-Armesto, Felipe. 2001. *Civilizations: Culture, Ambition, and the Transformation of Nature*. New York: The Free Press.

Finer, S.E. 1999. *The History of Government from the Earliest Times, Volume I: Ancient Monarchies and Empires*. New York: Oxford University Press.

Fleurbaey, Marc, and Philippe Michel. 2003. "Intertemporal Equity and the Extension of the Ramsey Criterion." *Journal of Mathematical Economics* 39: 777–802.

Fogel, Robert William. 2004. *The Escape from Hunger and Premature Death, 1700–2100*. Cambridge: Cambridge University Press.

Frankfurt, Harry G. 1988. *The Importance of What We Care About: Philosophical Essays*. Cambridge: Cambridge University Press.

Frazier, Robert L. 1994. "Act Utilitarianism and Decision Procedures." *Utilitas* 50: 253–256.

Frederick, Shane. 2003. "Measuring Intergenerational Time Preference: Are Future Lives Valued Less?" *The Journal of Risk and Uncertainty* 26, no. 1: 39–53.

Frederick, Shane. 2005. "Cognitive Reflection and Decision Making." *Journal of Economic Perspectives* 19, no. 4 (Fall): 25–42.

Frederick, Shane. 2006. "Valuing Future Life and Future Lives: A Framework for Understanding Discounting." *Journal of Economic Psychology* 27: 667–680.

Frederick, Shane, and George Loewenstein. 1999. "Hedonic Adaptation." In *Well-Being: The Foundations of Hedonic Psychology*, edited by Daniel Kahneman, Ed Diener, and Norbert Schwarz, 302–329. New York: Russell Sage Foundation.

Frederick, Shane, George Loewenstein, and Ted O'Donoghue. 2002. "Time Discounting and Time Preference: A Critical Review." *Journal of Economic Literature* 40, no. 2: 351–401.

Frey, Bruno S., and Alois Stutzer. 2000. "Happiness, Economy and Institutions." *The Economic Journal* 110, no. 466: 918–938.

Frey, Bruno S., and Alois Stutzer. 2002. *Happiness and Economics*. Princeton and Oxford: Princeton University Press.

Friedman, Benjamin M. 2006. *The Moral Consequences of Economic Growth*. New York: Vintage.

Galston, William A. 2002. *Liberal Pluralism: The Implications of Value Pluralism for Political Theory and Practice*. Cambridge: Cambridge University Press.

Glazer, Amihai, and Lawrence S. Rothenberg. 2005. *Why Government Succeeds and Why It Fails*. Cambridge: Harvard University Press.

Goodin, Robert. 1995. *Utilitarianism as a Public Philosophy*. Cambridge: Cambridge University Press.

Gollier, Christian. 2013. *Pricing the Planet's Future: The Economics of Discounting in an Uncertain World*. Princeton: Princeton University Press.

Goodin, Robert E. 1995. *Utilitarianism as a Public Philosophy*. New York: Cambridge University Press.

Goodin, Robert E., Bruce Headey, Ruud Muffels, and Henk–Jan Dirven. 1999. *The Real Worlds of Welfare Capitalism*. Cambridge: Cambridge University Press.

Greiner, Alfred, Willi Semmler, and Gang Gong. 2005. *The Forces of Economic Growth: A Time Series Perspective*. Princeton: Princeton University Press.

Grier, Kevin B., and Gordon Tullock. 1989. "An Empirical Analysis of Cross National Economic Growth." *Journal of Monetary Economics* 22 (September): 259–76.

Griffin, James. 2008. *On Human Rights*. Oxford: Oxford University Press.

Harding, Robin, Richard McGregor, and Gabriel Muller. "U.S. Public Investment Falls to Lowest Level Since War." *Financial Times*, November 3, 2013.

Hayek, Friedrich A. 1991. *The Fatal Conceit: The Errors of Socialism*. Chicago: University of Chicago Press.

Heal, Geoffrey. 1998. *Valuing the Future: Economic Theory and Sustainability*. New York: Columbia University Press.

Heath, Joseph. 2013. "The Structure of Intergenerational Cooperation." *Philosophy and Public Affairs* 41, no. 1: 31–66.

Helliwell, John F. 2002. "How's Life? Combining Individual and National Variables to Explain Subjective Well–Being." NBER Working Paper No. 9065.

Helpman, Elhanan. 2004. *The Mystery of Economic Growth*. Cambridge: The President and Fellows of Harvard College.

Hoehn, John P., and Alan Randall. 1989. "Too Many Proposals Pass the Cost–Benefit Test." *American Economic Review* 79, no. 3 (June): 544–551.

Hooker, Brad. 2000. *Ideal Code, Real World: A Rule-Consequentialist Theory of Morality*. Oxford: Clarendon Press.

Howard-Snyder, Frances. 1997. "The Rejection of Objective Consequentialism." *Utilitas* 9, no. 2 (July): 241-248.

Huberman, Michael, and Chris Minns. 2007. "The Times They Are Not Changin': Days and Hours of Work in Old and New Worlds, 1870-2000." *Explorations in Economic History* 44: 538-567.

Huemer, Michael. 2005. *Ethical Intuitionism*. Palgrave Macmillan.

Huntington, Samuel P. 1996. *The Clash of Civilizations?: The Debate*. New York: Foreign Affairs.

Huntington, Samuel P. 2011. *The Clash of Civilizations and the Remaking of World Order*. New York: Touchstone.

Hurka, Thomas. 1993. *Perfectionism*. Oxford: Oxford University Press.

Hurley, Paul. 2009. *Beyond Consequentialism*. Oxford: Oxford University Press.

Ipcher, John, and Homa Zarghamee. 2011. "Happiness and Time Preference: The Effect of Positive Affect in a Random-Assignment Experiment." *American Economic Review* 101, no. 7 (December): 3109-3129.

Jones, Charles I., and Peter J. Klenow. 2016. "Beyond GDP?: Welfare Across Countries and Time." *American Economic Review* 106, no. 9: 2426-2457.

Jones-Lee, M.W., ed. 1982. *The Value of Life and Safety*. North-Holland Publishing Company.

Kagan, Shelley. 1998. *Normative Ethics*. Boulder: Westview Press.

Kagan, Shelly. 2011. "Do I Make a Difference?" *Philosophy and Public Affairs* 39, no. 2: 105-141.

Kahneman, Daniel, Paul Slovic, and Amos Tversky, eds. 1982. *Judgment Under Uncertainty: Heuristics and Biases*. Cambridge: Cambridge University Press.

Kahneman, Daniel, et al., 2006. "Would You Be Happier if You Were Richer? A Focusing Illusion." *Science* 312: 1908–1910.

Keeley, Lawrence H. 1996. *War Before Civilization: The Myth of the Peaceful Savage*. New York: Oxford University Press.

Kekes, John. 1993. *The Morality of Pluralism*. Princeton: Princeton University Press.

Kenny, Charles. 1999. "Does Growth Cause Happiness, or Does Happiness Cause Growth?" *Kyklos* 52, no. 1: 3–25.

Kessler, Ronald C., Richard H. Price, and Camille B. Wortman. 1985. "Social Factors in Psychopathology: Stress, Social Support, and Coping Processes." *Annual Review of Psychology* 36: 531–572.

Kolmar, Martin, and Hendrik Rommeswinkel. 2013. "On General Arguments about the Cluelessness Objection." Unpublished manuscript. University of St. Gallen.

Koopmans, Tjalling. 1960. "Stationary Ordinal Utility and Impatience." *Econometrica* 28: 287–309.

Kydland, Finn E., and Edward C. Prescott. 1977. "Rules Rather Than Discretion: The Inconsistency of Optimal Plans." *Journal of Political Economy* 85, no. 3 (June): 473–492.

Lakner, Christoph, and Branko Milanovic. 2014. "Global Income Distribution: From the Fall of the Berlin Wall to the Great Recession." VOX, CEPR's Policy Portal. Accessed 27 May.

Lane, Robert E. 1998. "The Joyless Market Economy." In *Economics, Values, and Organization*, edited by Avner Ben–Ner and Louis Putterman, 461–490. New York: Cambridge University Press.

Lang, Gerald. 2008. "Consequentialism, Cluelessness, and Indifference." *The Journal of Value Inquiry* 42: 477–485.

LeBlanc, Steven A. 2003. *Constant Battles: The Myth of the Peaceful, Noble Savage*. New York: Macmillan.

Lehman, Darrin R., Camille B. Wortman, and Alan F. Williams. 1987. "Long-Term Effects of Losing a Spouse or Child in a Motor Vehicle Crash." *Journal of Personality and Social Psychology* 52, no. 1: 218–231.

Lenman, James. 2000. "Consequentialism and Cluelessness." *Philosophy and Public Affairs* 29, no. 4: 342–370.

Levinson, Arik. 2013. "Happiness, Behavioral Economics, and Public Policy." NBER Working Paper No. 19329.

Lind, Robert C., Kenneth J. Arrow, Gordon R. Corey, Partha Dasgupta, Amartya K. Sen, Thomas Stauffer, Joseph E. Stiglitz, and J.A. Stockfisch. 1982. *Discounting for Time and Risk in Energy Policy*. New York: Resources for the Future.

Lindert, Peter H. 2004. *Growing Public, Vol. I*. Cambridge: Cambridge University Press.

Lucas, Robert E. 1988. "On the Mechanics of Economic Development." *Journal of Monetary Economics* 22: 3–42.

Lyons, David. 1965. *Forms and Limits of Utilitarianism*. Oxford: Clarendon Press.

MacAskill, William. 2014. "Normative Uncertainty." PhD diss., St. Anne's College, Oxford University.

Mackie, J.L. 1985. *Persons and Values: Selected Papers, Vol. II*. Oxford: Clarendon Press.

Mahoney, Paul. 2001. "The Common Law and Economic Growth: Hayek Might Be Right." *Journal of Legal Studies* 30, no. 2: 503–525

Mason, Elinor. 2004. "Consequentialism and the Principle of Indifference." *Utilitas* 16, no. 3 (November): 317–321.

Meade, James E. 1962. "The Effect of Savings on Consumption in a State of Steady Growth." *Review of Economic Studies* 29, no. 3 (June): 227–234.

Melko, Matthew. 1969. *The Nature of Civilizations*. Boston: Sargent.

Meyer, C. Buf, and Shelley E. Taylor. 1986. "Adjustment to Rape." *Journal of Personality and Social Psychology* 50, no. 6: 1226–1234.

Mill, John Stuart. 1958 [1861]. *Considerations on Representative Government*. New York: Bobbs–Merrill.

Mill, John Stuart. 1969 [1852]. "Whewell on Moral Philosophy." In *Essays on Ethics, Religion and Society*, edited by J.M. Robson, 165–202. Toronto: University of Toronto Press.

Mischel, Walter, Yuichi Shoda, and Monica L. Rodriguez. 1989. "Delay of Gratification in Children." *Science*, May 26, 1989.

Moffitt, Terrie E., et al. 2011. "A Gradient of Childhood Self-Control Predicts Health, Wealth, and Public Safety," *Proceedings of the National Academy of Sciences of the United States of America* 108, no. 7: 2693–2698.

Moller, Dan, 2011. "Wealth, Disability, and Happiness." *Philosophy and Public Affairs* 39, no. 2: 177–206.

Moriarty, Jeffrey. 2005. "The Epistemological Argument Against Desert." *Utilitas* 17, no. 2: 205–221.

Myers, David G. 2000. "The Funds, Friends, and Faith of Happy People." *American Psychologist* 55, no. 1: 56–67.

Nagel, Thomas. 1986. *The View from Nowhere*. Oxford: Oxford University Press.

Nefsky, Julia. 2012. "Consequentialism and the Problem of Collective Harm: Reply to Kagan." *Philosophy and Public Affairs* 39, no. 4: 365–395.

Norcross, Alastair. 1990. "Consequentialism and the Unforeseeable Future." *Analysis* 50: 253–256.

North, Douglass C. 1981. *Structure and Change in Economic History*. W.W. Norton & Co.

North, Douglass C., and Robert Paul Thomas. 1976. *The Rise of the Western World: A New Economic History*. Cambridge: Cambridge University Press.

Nozick, Robert. 1974. *Anarchy, State, and Utopia*. New York: Basic Books.

O'Driscoll, Gerald P. Jr., and Mario Rizzo. 1996. *The Economics of Time and Ignorance*. Routledge.

Olson, Mancur. 1984. *The Rise and Decline of Nations*. New Haven: Yale University Press.

Oswald, Andrew J. 1997. "Happiness and Economic Performance." *The Economic Journal* 107, no. 445: 1815–1831.

Oulton, Nicholas. 2012. "Hooray for GDP!" Unpublished manuscript. London School of Economics.

Parfit, Derek. 1984. *Reasons and Persons*. Oxford: Clarendon Press.

Parfit, Derek. 1986. "Overpopulation and the Quality of Life." In *Applied Ethics*, edited by Peter Singer. New York: Oxford University Press.

Parfit, Derek. 2011. *On What Matters, Volumes I and II*. Oxford: Oxford University Press.

Persson, Torsten, and Guido Tabellini. 1994. "Is Inequality Harmful for Growth?" *American Economic Review* 84, no. 3: 600–621.

Pettit, Philip. 1997. "The Consequentialist Perspective." *In Three Methods of Ethics: A Debate*, edited by Marcia Baron, 92–174. Malden: Blackwell.

Phelps, Edmund S. 1961. "The Golden Rule of Accumulation: A Fable for Growthmen." *American Economic Review* 51, no. 4 (September): 638–643.

Pinker, Steven. 2018. *Enlightenment Now: The Case for Reason, Science, Humanism, and Progress*. New York: Viking Press.

Posner, Richard A. 2004. *Catastrophe: Risk and Response*. New York: Oxford University Press.

Price, Colin. 1993. *Time, Discounting, and Value*. Oxford: Blackwell.

Pritchett, Lant. 1997. "Diverge, Big Time." *Journal of Economic Perspectives* 11, no. 3: 3–17.

Quine, Willard van Orman. 1953. *From a Logical Point of View*. Cambridge: Harvard University Press.

Railton, Peter. 1984. "Alienation, Consequentialism, and the Demands of Morality." *Philosophy and Public Affairs* 13: 134–71.

Ramsey, Frank. 1928. "A Mathematical Theory of Saving." *Economic Journal* 38: 543–559.

Rand, Ayn. 1967. *Capitalism: The Unknown Ideal*. New York: Signet Books.

Rangel, Antonio. 2000. "Forward and Backward Intergenerational Goods: A Theory of Intergenerational Exchange." NBER Working Paper No. 7518.

Rawls, John. 1993. *Political Liberalism*. New York: Columbia University Press.

Rawls, John. 1999. *A Theory of Justice*. Cambridge: Belknap Press of Harvard University Press.

Regan, Donald. 1980. *Utilitarianism and Cooperation*. Oxford: Clarendon Press.

Rees, William E. 2003. "Energy, Evolution and Civilization: The Global Context." Invited paper to Energy, Environment and Society: Making Choices, the 2003 Annual Symposium of the Royal Society of Canada. Ottawa, Ontario, November 25.

Romer, David. 2000. *Advanced Macroeconomics*. New York: Mcgraw-Hill.

Romer, Paul M. 1986. "Increasing Returns and Long-Run Growth." *Journal of Political Economy* 94: 1002-1037.

Romer, Paul M. 1990. "Endogenous Technological Change." *Journal of Political Economy* 98: S71-S102.

Rorty, Richard. 1989. *Contingency, Irony, and Solidarity*. Cambridge: Cambridge University Press.

Sacks, Daniel W., Betsey Stevenson, and Justin Wolfers. 2010. "Subjective Well-Being, Income, Economic Development, and Growth." NBER Working Paper No. 16441.

Sakai, Toyotaka. 2003. "Intergenerational Preferences and Sensitivity to the Present." *Economics Bulletin* 4, no. 26: 1-5.

Sala-i-Martin, Xavier X. 1997. "I Just Ran Two Million Regressions." *American Economic Review* 87, no. 2 (May): 178-183.

Scarre, Geoffrey. 1996. *Utilitarianism*. New York: Routledge.

Scheffler, Samuel. 1982. *The Rejection of Consequentialism*. Oxford: Clarendon Press.

Schneewind, J.B. 1977. *Sidgwick's Ethics and Victorian Moral Philosophy*. Oxford: Clarendon Press.

Schwarz, Norbert, and Fritz Strack. 1999. "Reports of Subjective Well-Being: Judgmental Processes and their Methodological Implications." In *Well-Being: The Foundations of Hedonic Psychology*, edited by Daniel Kahneman, Ed Diener, and Norbert Schwarz, 61-84. New York: Russell Sage Foundation.

Scully, Matthew. 2003. *Dominion: The Power of Man, the Suffering of Animals, and the Call to Mercy*. New York: St. Martin's.

Sen, Amartya. 1984. *Resources, Values and Development*. Cambridge: Harvard University Press.

Sidgwick, Henry. 1962 [1906]. *The Methods of Ethics*. Chicago: The University of Chicago Press.

Singer, Peter. 1003. *Practical Ethics*. Cambridge: Cambridge University Press.

Slote, Michael. 1992. *From Morality to Virtue*. Oxford: Oxford University Press.

Smart, J.C.C., and Bernard Williams. 1973. *Utilitarianism: For and Against*. Cambridge: Cambridge University Press.

Solow, Robert M. 1956. "A Contribution to the Theory of Economic Growth." *Quarterly Journal of Economics* 70, no. 1: 65-94.

Solow, Robert M. 1957. "Technical Change and the Aggregate Production Function." *The Review of Economics and Statistics* 39, no. 3: 312-320.

Solow, Robert M. 1974. "The Economics of Resources or the Resources of Economics." *American Economic Review* 64: 1-14.

Stanczyk, Lucas. 2012. "Productive Justice." *Philosophy and Public Affairs* 40, no. 2.

Stroebe, Margaret S., Robert O. Hansson, Wolfgang Stroebe, and Henk Schut, eds. 2001. *Handbook of Bereavement Research: Consequences, Coping, and Care*. Washington, D.C.: American Psychological Association.

Spolaore, Enrico, and Romain Wacziarg. 2013. "How Deep are the Roots of Economic Development?" *Journal of Economic Literature* 51, no. 2: 325–369.

Stevenson, Betsey, and Justin Wolfers. 2008. "Economic Growth and Subjective Well-Being: Reassessing the Easterlin Paradox." *Brookings Papers on Economic Activity* (Spring): 1–102.

Stevenson, Betsey, and Justin Wolfers. 2013. "Subjective Well-Being and Income: Is There Any Evidence of Satiation?" NBER Working Paper No. 18992.

"Symposia: New Growth Theory." 1994. *Journal of Economic Perspectives* 8, no. 1: 3–72.

Temkin, Larry S. 1987. "Intransitivity and the Mere Addition Paradox." *Philosophy and Public Affairs* 25, no. 3 (Spring): 175–210.

Temkin, Larry S. 1996. "A Continuum Argument for Intransitivity." *Philosophy and Public Affairs* 25, no. 3 (Summer): 175–210.

Temple, Jonathan. 1999. "The New Growth Evidence." *Journal of Economic Literature* 37 (March): 112–156.

Toynbee, Arnold J. 1987. *A Study of History, Vols. 1–2*. New York: Oxford University Press.

Tsai, Kellee. 2006. "The Wenzhou and Kerala Models." *Indian Journal of Economics and Business* (Special Issue China & India): 47–67.

Uzawa, Hirofumi. 1965. "Optimum Technical Change in an Aggregative Model of Economic Growth." *International Economic Review* 6: 18–31.

Vallentyne, Peter. 1993. "Utilitarianism and Infinite Utility." *Australasian Journal of Philosophy* 71: 212–217.

Vallentyne, Peter. 1995. "Infinite Utility, Anonymity and Person-Centeredness." *Australasian Journal of Philosophy* 73: 212–217.

Vallentyne, Peter, and Shelly Kagan. 1997. "Infinite Value and Finitely Additive Value Theory." *Journal of Philosophy* 94: 5–26.

Van Inwagen, Peter. 1983. *An Essay on Free Will*. Oxford: Clarendon Press.

Väyrynen, Pekka. 2006. "Moral Generalism: Enjoy in Moderation." *Ethics* 116, no. 4 (July): 707–741.

Venkatraman, Triyakshana. 2009. "The Kerala Paradox." *Indian Journal of Economics and Business* 8, no. 1: 43–54.

Wall, Steven. 1998. *Liberalism, Perfectionism, and Restraint*. Cambridge: Cambridge University Press.

Weiss, Ron. 1987. "Wrongful Birth and Wrongful Life: In Search of a Logical Consistency." *Annual Survey of American Law* 2: 507–522.

Weitzman, Martin L. 1998. "Why the Far–Distant Future Should Be Discounted at Its Lowest Possible Rate." *Journal of Environmental Economics and Management* 36: 201–208.

Weitzman, Martin L. 2001. "Gamma Discounting." *American Economic Review* 91, no. 1: 260–271.

Weitzman, Martin L. 2012. "The Ramsey Discounting Formula for a Hidden–State Stochastic Growth Process." NBER Working Paper No. 18157.

Wenar, Leif. 2013. "The Nature of Claim Rights." *Ethics* 123, no. 2 (January): 202–229.

Wildasin, David E. 1988. "Indirect Distributional Effects in Benefit–Cost Analysis of Small Projects." *The Economic Journal* 98 (September): 801–807.

Williamson, Timothy. 2003. "Vagueness in Reality." In *Oxford Handbook of Metaphysics*, edited by Michael Loux and Dean W. Zimmerman, 690–716. Oxford: Oxford University Press.

Wirtz, Phillip W., and Adale V. Harrell. 1987. "The Effects of Threatening Versus Non–Threatening Previous Live Events on Levels of Fear in Rape Victims." *Violence and Victims* 2, no. 2: 89–98.

Wolf, Susan. 1982. "Moral Saints." *Journal of Philosophy* 79: 419–39.

Wortman, Camille B., and Roxane Cohen Silver. 1987. "Coping with Irrevocable Loss." *In Cataclysms, Crises, and Catastrophes: Psychology in Action*, edited by Gary VandenBos and Brenda Bryant, 185–235. Washington, D.C.: American Psychological Association.

Wortman, Camille B., Collette Sheedy, Vicki Gluhoski, and Ron Kessler. 1992. "Stress, Coping, and Health: Conceptual Issues and Directions for Future Research." *In Hostility, Coping, and Health*, edited by Howard S. Friedman, 227–256. Washington, D.C.: American Psychological Association.

A Stubborn Attachment to Yonas

One theme of *Stubborn Attachments* is that economic growth in the wealthier countries has positive spillover effects for poorer individuals around the world. If you think of the publication of this book as a form of economic growth/GDP enhancement, I want to boost its positive global effects. I also argue in *Stubborn Attachments* that we should be more charitable and altruistic at the margin. That includes me!

So, having written *Stubborn Attachments*, I now wish to live the book, so to speak. **I am donating the earnings from the book to a man I met in Ethiopia on a fact-finding trip earlier this year.** I shall call him Yonas (not his real name).

He is a man of modest means, but he aspires to open his own travel business. He has a young and growing family, and also a mother to support. He is also hoping to buy a larger house to accommodate his growing family. In his life, he faces stresses—financial and otherwise—that I have never had to confront. When I visited his home, his wife had just had a new baby girl, but Yonas's income depends on the vicissitudes of tourist demand, and by American standards it is in any case low.

I met Yonas when he served as my travel guide around Lalibela. I spent a full day with him touring the underground, rock-hewn stone churches of that city. He struck me as reliable, conscientious, well informed, and I was impressed by the quality of his English, which he had acquired on his own. He also took me by his village to meet his family, and they performed a coffee ceremony for me, cooking freshly ground coffee beans (it was delicious, something I had never imagined). Based on my impressions from that day, I believe an investment in Yonas will help his entire family and perhaps his broader community as well. Since then, he and I have kept in touch by email.

As another way of living the content of my book, I will be sending the funds via Stripe, Stripe Press being the publisher of this book. Stripe, a technology and payments company that builds economic infrastructure for the internet, really has made it easy to send money across borders, thereby helping to knit the whole world together. I hope someday Yonas is able to start his travel business, or whatever else he may wish to do, with the help of Stripe Atlas.

I suppose this means I will remain stubbornly attached to Yonas. And with the publication of this book, Stripe Press is now stubbornly attached to me.

—Tyler Cowen